COOK AND DEAL

A collection of favorite recipes
and
favorite bridge hands

by *DJ Cook*

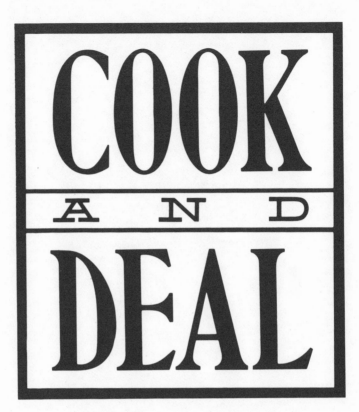

My sincere appreciation to the many friends
who have made this book possible.

P.O. Box 3238
Beach Station
Vero Beach, Florida 32960

ISBN: 0-939114-53-4

Printed in the United States of America
Wimmer Brothers Fine Printing and Lithography
Memphis, Tennessee 38118

"Cookbooks of Distinction"™

A note to you from the author of COOK AND DEAL:

There are more than 12 million bridge players in North America.* All of them eat . . . and most of them cook! While waiting for the soufflé to rise or the strawberry salad to freeze, I hope you will enjoy studying some of my favorite bridge-teaching hands.

While the "four decks" of 208 recipes include favorites of many of my students, I have made each one on my own, can attest to its accuracy and excellence, and well understand why it has attained most-favored status. I invite you to share and enjoy these treasured recipes, old and new, easy and distinctive.

Likewise, the "single deck" of 52 bridge hands comprises favorites not only of mine, but also many of my students. From the thousands of bridge hands that I have used since 1947 in teaching the Goren System, these 52 hands illustrate the basic principles of Standard American Bridge. The Goren principles of bidding and play presented here should make it possible for anyone to play acceptable bridge in any company. Serious study of these hands could well improve your game and make you a welcome player in any foursome.

As you prepare a favorite recipe for your bridge group, sharpen your bidding and play by studying these challenging bridge hands.

DJ Cook
Life Master #236

*The American Contract Bridge League
National Headquarters
Memphis, Tennessee

Dedicated to my sons

With admiration and affection

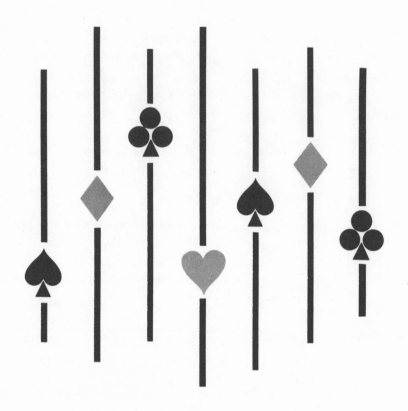

TABLE OF CONTENTS

PART I

RECIPES . . . "FOUR DECKS"

TABLE OF CONTENTS

PART II

BRIDGE HANDS... "ONE DECK"

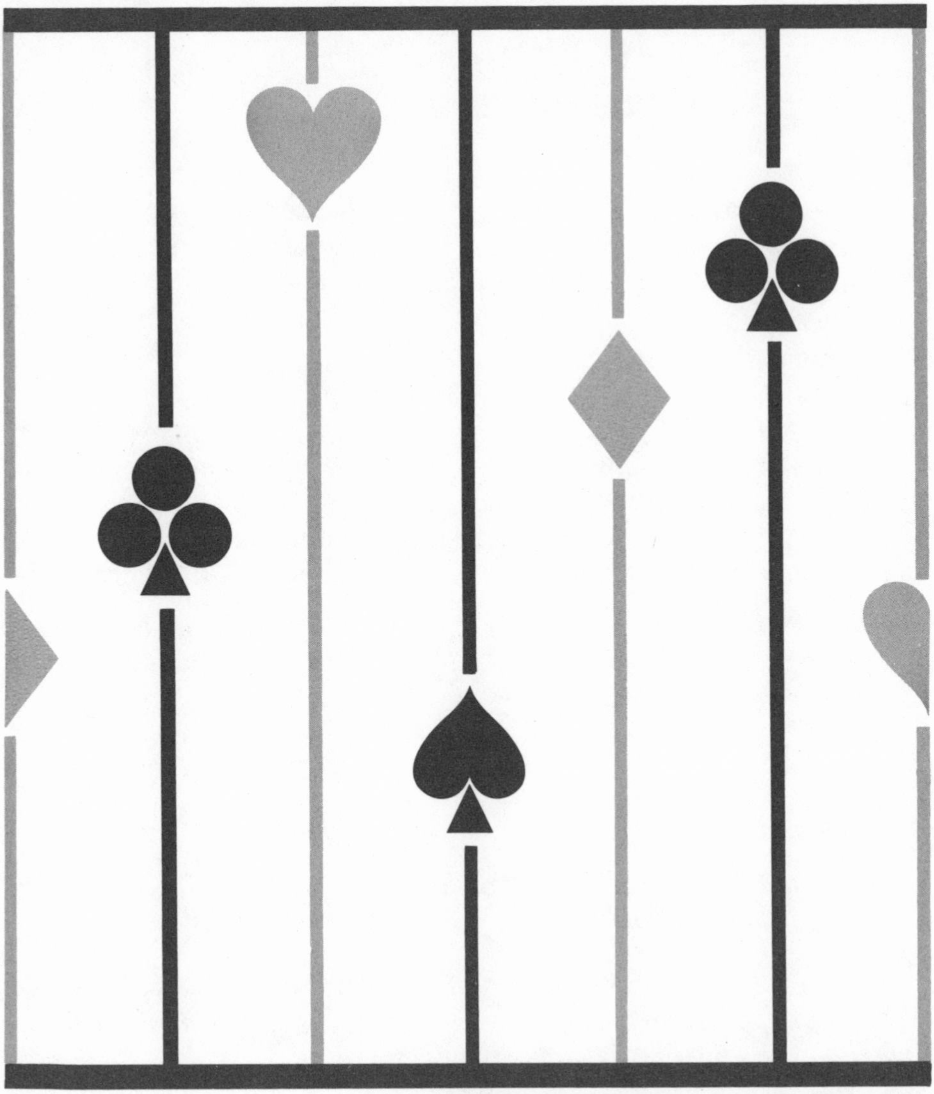

APPETIZERS

ARTICHOKE HEART SPREAD

A conversation piece

1 (14-ounce) can artichoke hearts
1 cup Hellmann's mayonnaise
6 ounces Parmesan cheese, freshly grated
2 or 3 dashes Tabasco
Pinch cayenne pepper
Salt to taste

Preheat oven to 350 degrees. Drain artichoke hearts well; chop fine. Mix with mayonnaise, cheese and seasoning. Blend thoroughly. Pour into an 8 inch square baking pan or a quiche dish and bake for 30 minutes. Serve hot with assorted crackers. Serves 12.

Gerald Stelter, M.D.
Neenah, Wisconsin

BLACK MAGIC

A do-ahead hors d'oeuvre that will be the hit of the party

1 (8 ounce) package cream cheese, softened
⅔ cup sour cream
1 large onion, grated
4 or 5 hard-cooked eggs, grated
1 (3½ ounce) jar Romanoff black lumpfish, Icelandic caviar

Combine cream cheese and sour cream; beat until smooth. Spread in an 8-inch quiche dish or shallow serving dish to make an even layer. Add a layer of grated onion; then a layer of grated eggs. Cover. Chill 3 hours or more, or overnight. At party time, top with caviar, distributing it to the edge of the dish. Serve with toast points or crackers. Serves 10.

Dorothy Kohler
Atlanta, Georgia

BEGGARS BOURSIN AU POIVRE

As good as the real thing and maybe better!

1 (8 ounce) package cream cheese, softened
⅓ cup sour cream or King Sour
¼ cup unsalted butter, softened
1 clove garlic, pressed
1 tablespoon dried chives
1 teaspoon dried parsley, soaked in a little water and drained
½ teaspoon Fines Herbes (Spice Island)
Pinch of salt
Pinch of fresh ground pepper
1 tablespoon lemon pepper marinade

In a medium size bowl mix all ingredients but lemon pepper marinade. Blend until smooth. Refrigerate 30 minutes or more, until mixture is firm. Sprinkle lemon pepper on a sheet of wax paper. Using hands, mold cheese into a round, flat shape. Roll cheese in the lemon pepper until well covered. Cover and refrigerate until ready to serve. Serve with assorted crackers. Makes 1 cup cheese spread.

BURGUNDY BEEF PATTIES

Your guests will eat three or four or MORE each . . . can you believe it?

1½ pounds ground chuck, ground twice
2 tablespoons chili sauce
¼ teaspoon Worcestershire sauce
½ teaspoon minced onion
½ teaspoon prepared mustard
¼ teaspoon horseradish
¼ cup red Burgundy wine
Salt and pepper to taste
50-55 tiny buns

Combine ingredients well and chill. Form into patties the size of a 50 cent piece. Flatten. Place on cookie sheet and broil 2 minutes on each side. Serve in tiny buns. Makes 50-55 patties.

This recipe from the Woman's Athletic Club of Chicago Cook Book is included by special permission of the club.

BLACK-EYED PEA DIP

So Southern and truly delicious

1 pound smoked ham hocks
3 tablespoons bacon drippings
4 tablespoons grated onion
1 teaspoon salt
½ teaspoon pepper
1 pound frozen black-eyed peas
1 (10 ounce) can Ro-tel or Ashley tomatoes with green chilies
Very small pieces cooked ham (optional)
Strips of avocado dipped in lemon juice for garnish

Place ham hocks, bacon drippings, onion, salt and pepper in a dutch oven; add about 6 cups water, just enough to barely cover. Cover and cook over low heat for 1½ hours. Add black-eyed peas and ½ can tomatoes with green chilies. Cover and simmer for 4 hours. Remove from heat; drain, reserving 1 to 1½ cups liquid. Place peas and ½ can tomatoes with chilies in a blender with a little of the liquid. (A food processor may be used also.) Blend until smooth, adding more liquid if it is too thick. Add ham if used. Serve warm in a chafing dish or a 9 inch quiche dish with Fritos or Doritos. Garnish with avocado slices. Makes 2 cups dip. Serves 12.

Becky Alexander
Vero Beach, Florida

CURRY DIP FOR FRESH VEGETABLES

Excllent flavor

1 cup mayonnaise
1 teaspoon curry powder
1 teaspoon tarragon vinegar
1 clove garlic, pressed
1 teaspoon horseradish
1 teaspoon grated onion

Mix ingredients together and surround with crisp raw vegetables. This dip looks especially pretty in a hollowed-out red cabbage.

Blanche Evans
Vero Beach, Florida

MEXICAN ALARM

Olé

A great dip!

3 pounds ground chuck, coarsely ground
1 package 2 Alarm-Chili
1 (8 ounce) can tomato sauce
2 cans water
1 (16 ounce) can refried beans
1 (14 ounce) can tamales
2 cups sharp cheddar cheese, grated
2 cups avocado dip (page 21)
1 cup spring onions, finely chopped
2 cups sour cream

Sear meat until grayish color. Add 2 Alarm-Chili package omitting the masa flour and only use ½ of the package of cayenne pepper. Stir in tomato sauce and water; add refried beans and tamales. Cook over low heat until tamales have dissolved, about 20-25 minutes; stir frequently. Put in 3-quart casserole, cover with cheese. Bake in preheated 350 degree oven for 20 minutes, or until hot. To serve, place 1 cup avocado dip in the center of the casserole, sprinkle with ½ cup chopped onions and put dollops of sour cream around the edges. Add remaining avocado dip, onions and sour cream when needed. Serve with tortilla chips. Dip may be frozen prior to baking. Makes 11 cups of dip. Serve 40-50.

Cookie Smith
Vero Beach, Florida

SPINACH DIP

Dunkers' Delight

1 (10 ounce) package frozen, chopped spinach
½ cup sour cream
½ cup mayonnaise
½ cup chopped green onions
½ cup chopped fresh parsley
1 clove garlic, crushed
½ teaspoon salt
1 teaspoon dill weed
1 teaspoon Beau Monde
1 tablespoon fresh lemon juice, to taste

Drain spinach thoroughly; blot dry. Mix all ingredients with spinach. Refrigerate several hours. Serve with crackers or potato chips. Also good with any fresh vegetables: celery sticks, carrots, radishes, cauliflower or cucumbers. Makes 2 cups.

Helen Walters
Richmond, Virginia

CRANBERRY LIVER PÂTÉ

Easy to fix and a joy to eat

1 pound Braunschweiger sausage
1 (8 ounce) package cream cheese
½ cup butter
¼ cup cranberry juice
2 teaspoons curry powder
½ teaspoon thyme
½ teaspoon marjoram
¼ teaspoon salt

Have all ingredients at room temperature. Mash Braunschweiger in a food processor or by hand; beat in cream cheese and butter. Blend in cranberry juice and seasonings. Pack into a crock, cover tightly and refrigerate for 2 days. Serve with thin slices toasted French bread, fingers of Swiss cheese or stone ground wheat crackers. Cornichons (gherkins in vinegar) are a fine accompaniment. May freeze. Makes 3½ cups.

Sally Brooker
Mountain Lake Club, Lake Wales, Florida

CHUTNEY CHEESE SPREAD

Really good!

2 (8 ounce) packages cream cheese
½ cup chutney, chopped fine
1½ to 2 teaspoons curry powder
½ teaspoon dry mustard
½ cup toasted chopped almonds

Soften cream cheese to room temperature; mix with remaining ingredients. Store in covered jar in the refrigerator. Improves with age and keeps for weeks. Serve with crackers or Pita bread.

Pita Bread:
Preheat oven to 250 degrees. Split and tear bread into good size bite pieces. Brush with melted butter. Sprinkle with oregano. Bake until golden brown, 45 to 60 minutes. This will keep for weeks in a tin.

Gidge Barry
New Canaan, Connecticut

HOT CRAB AMANDINE

Good! Good!!

1 (8 ounce) package cream cheese
1 tablespoon milk
1 tablespoon dry sherry
1 tablespoon horseradish
Dash freshly ground pepper
1 (7 ounce) can crabmeat
Almonds, sliced

Preheat oven to 350 degrees. Soften cream cheese with milk, sherry, horseradish and pepper. Add crabmeat and mix well. Place in an 8-inch quiche dish and sprinkle top with sliced almonds. Bake 15 minutes, or until bubbly. Serve with triscuits. Serves 10 to 12.

Sissy Brophy
Gross Pointe Shores, Michigan

CRABMEAT DIP

Very popular

1 can crabmeat or ½ pound fresh crabmeat
1 cup small curd cottage cheese
¼ cup Hellmann's mayonnaise
1 tablespoon onion, grated
1 tablespoon capers
Salt and pepper to taste

Combine all ingredients. Chill several hours before serving. Serve with triscuits. Serves 8.

Mary Tatham
Tequesta, Florida

EGGS EVERGLADES

Elegant appetizer

1½ cups chicken broth
1 teaspoon curry powder
2 envelopes unflavored gelatin
4 hard-cooked eggs,chopped
1½ cups Hellmann's mayonnaise
Paprika
Caviar (optional)

Heat 1 cup of broth; dissolve curry powder in broth. Dissolve gelatin in remaining ½ cup broth. When broth is cool, add gelatin mixture. Add eggs. Blend in blender, add mayonnaise and reblend. Pour into a 3-cup mold, rinsed with cold water; refrigerate. Unmold when set, sprinkle with paprika, and serve with triscuits. Optional: Use a ring mold. Place a small bowl in the center of the ring and fill with black caviar. Serves 14 to 16.

Lazelle Rafferty
Little Compton, Rhode Island

HOT CHEESE DIP WITH APPLE SLICES

Unusual . . . delicious . . . always gets raves

6 slices bacon
1 (8 ounce) package cream cheese
2 cups shredded Cheddar cheese
6 tablespoons cream
1 teaspoon Worcestershire sauce
¼ teaspoon dry mustard
¼ teaspoon onion salt
6 to 8 dashes Tabasco
Unpared apples, cut into very thin wedges
Lemon juice

Cut bacon into ¼ inch slices; sauté until crisp and drain on absorbent paper. In the top of a double boiler, combine cream cheese, Cheddar cheese, cream, Worcestershire sauce, mustard, onion salt and Tabasco. Heat over simmering water, stirring occasionally, until cheese melts and mixture is hot. Add bacon pieces. Use this as a dip for apple slices which have been dipped in lemon juice. The dip may be served in a chafing dish and will hold well for several hours if stirred occasionally. If mixture becomes too thick, more cream may be added. Red Delicious apples are very good with this dip. Makes about 2 cups.

Elaine Putney
Vero Beach, Florida

ROJAK PETIS

(Indonesian Peanut Dip)
Something Special

⅔ cup crunchy peanut butter
6 tablespoons firmly packed dark brown sugar
½ cup lemon juice
4 tablespoons chili sauce
1 teaspoon soy sauce

Combine all ingredients. Store at room temperature for 24 hours. Refrigerate. Serve with celery and carrot sticks, iced cucumber strips, etc. Makes 1½ cups.

Bali Hyatt
Courtesy of Ruth Fuller
Mountain Lake Club, Lake Wales, Florida

GUACAMOLE PIE

Absolutely wonderful

Make the layers on a serving platter.

1st layer:
2 (15 ounce) cans refried beans mixed with 1 package taco seasoning

2nd layer:
2 cups avocado dip

3rd layer:
1 (4½ ounce) can chopped ripe olives
2 bunches green onions, chopped
1 small can green chiles, chopped
1 small jar chopped green olives with pimentos

Mix together.

4th layer:
2 peeled tomatoes, chopped, drained well

5th layer:
½ pound grated sharp Cheddar cheese; Sprinkle over top.

Drain everything *well*. This may be made a day ahead. Serve at room temperature. Place toasted tortilla chips or large corn chips around platter. Serves 20 to 25.

Avocado Dip:

3 avocados
2 tablespoons scraped onion
2 tablespoons lemon juice
¼ teaspoon chili powder
Few dashes Tabasco
Salt to taste
Hellmann's mayonnaise

Peel avocados and mash pulp with a fork. Add onion, lemon juice, chili powder, Tabasco and salt to taste. Spread a thin layer of mayonnaise over the top surface of the mixture. This seals out the air and prevents the avocado dip from turning dark. Mix mayonnaise into the spread just before adding the next layer.

Phyllis Holliday
Zionville, Indiana

ENGLISH MUFFIN CANAPÉ

Incredibly good

6 English muffins, separated
2 (4½ ounce) cans chopped ripe olives
1½ cups shredded white strong cheese or very sharp Cheddar
½ cup grated onion
½ cup Hellmann's mayonnaise
½ tablespoon curry powder
½ teaspoon salt

Mix all ingredients and pile on 12 muffin halves. Place on a cookie sheet and freeze. When frozen, place in baggies and return to freezer. To serve, cut each half muffin into 8 pieces. They are easier to cut when still a little frozen. Place on broiler pan and broil until bubbly. Makes 96 pieces.

Madeline Crawford
Vero Beach, Florida

LAYERED CRAB OR SHRIMP COCKTAIL SPREAD

Guests gather around this . . . it's a winner

12 ounces cream cheese, softened
1 tablespoon Worchestershire sauce
1 tablespoon fresh lemon juice
1 tablespoon grated onion
Pinch garlic salt
6 ounces chili sauce
8 ounces fresh crabmeat or shrimp, cut up
Dried parsley flakes

Blend together the cheese, Worchestershire sauce, lemon juice, onion and garlic salt. Spread mixture evenly in an 8-inch quiche dish or shallow serving dish. Spread chili sauce evenly over the first layer. Spread the crabmeat or cut up shrimp over the chili sauce. Sprinkle generously with dried parsley flakes. Cover with saran wrap and refrigerate a minimum of 12 hours. Serve with crackers. Serves 10 to 12.

Marie Feeney
Northbrook, Illinois

HOT CHIPPED BEEF DIP

Very easy and very good

1 (8 ounce) package cream cheese, softened
1 cup sour cream
1 (3 ounce) package dried beef, finely chopped
1 tablespoon onion, finely grated
¼ teaspoon black pepper
¼ teaspoon garlic salt
½ cup chopped pecans which have been sautéed in 2 tablespoons butter

Preheat oven to 350 degrees. Combine all ingredients except pecans. Mix well. Turn into a shallow serving dish. Top with pecans. Bake for 20 to 25 minutes. Serve hot with triscuits. Serves 10.

Frances Taylor
Kenilworth, Illinois

PÂTÉ EN GELÉE

A gem of a recipe

1 package unflavored gelatin
¼ cup water
1 (10½ ounce) can beef consommé
2 tablespoons dry sherry
½ pound liverwurst
1 (3 ounce) package cream cheese, softened
1 tablespoon parsley
1 tablespoon onion tops
1 tablespoon capers
3 tablespoons Worcestershire sauce
Dash nutmeg

Soak gelatin in cold water. Heat consommé, remove from heat and add gelatin. Cool. Add sherry. Put ½ inch of consommé mixture in a 2 cup mold, lightly greased. Refrigerate until congealed. Put remaining consommé in blender; add liverwurst, cream cheese, parsley, onion tops, capers, Worcestershire sauce and nutmeg. Blend on low speed, to start, and then at a higher speed until fluffy. Pour over congealed consommé and refrigerate. Serve with wafers, toast triangles or melba toast. Serves 12.

Patty Bennett
Wilmette, Illinois

TAMALE DIP

A happy hostess . . . guests too!

2 (15 ounce) cans chili without beans
4 (15 ounce) cans tamales, shucked and mashed
1 pound sharp Cheddar cheese, shredded
½ teaspoon cayenne pepper
1½ teaspoons salt
½ teaspoon white pepper
1½ tablespoons Worcestershire sauce

Put all ingredients in the top of a double boiler until dissolved and hot. Place in a chafing dish and serve with large corn chips. Serves 30 to 40.

Beverley Wood
Vero Beach, Florida

PARTY CHEESE BALLS

- 1 (8 ounce) package cream cheese, softened
- 1 pound sharp Cheddar cheese, shredded
- 4 ounces Roquefort or bleu cheese, crumbled
- 2 teaspoons finely grated onion
- 2 teaspoons Worcestershire sauce
- 2 tablespoons chopped stuffed olives
- Dash cayenne pepper
- 1 cup chopped pecans
- ½ cup parsley, minced

Combine all ingredients but pecans and parsley. Blend thoroughly. Chill several hours or overnight. Form into balls. Mix pecans and parsley on waxed paper. Roll cheese balls in this mixture until completely covered. Arrange on tray with assorted crackers and potato chips. Serves 16 to 20.

PARTY PIZZAS

Marvelous!

- 2 loaves party rye bread
- Salad oil
- 1 (10¾ ounce) can condensed tomato soup
- 1 (6 ounce) can tomato paste
- 1½ teaspoons ground oregano
- 1 teaspoon curry powder
- 12 ounces mozzarella cheese, shredded
- 3 (4 ounce) packages pepperoni, thinly sliced
- Parmesan cheese, grated

Preheat oven to 350 degrees. Brush bread with salad oil. Make sauce of soup, tomato paste, oregano and curry powder. Spread sauce on bread. Put mozzarella cheese over sauce. Add thin slices of pepperoni; sprinkle with Parmesan cheese. Bake for 15 minutes. To serve, cut in half after baking. To freeze: Place on cookie sheets. When frozen, transfer to plastic bags or freezer containers. Bring back to room temperature before baking. Makes 60 whole slices.

Lazelle Rafferty
Little Compton, Rhode Island

CRAB PÂTÉ

An excellent combination of flavors

1 (10¾ ounce) can cream of mushroom soup, undiluted
1 envelope unflavored gelatin
3 tablespoons cold water
1 (8 ounce) package cream cheese, softened
¾ cup mayonnaise
1 small onion, grated
1 cup celery, chopped
½ pound fresh crabmeat or 1 can crabmeat
Dash Worcestershire sauce
Dash seasoned salt
Parsley for garnish

Heat soup. Soften gelatin in cold water and dissolve in hot soup. Remove from heat and combine with cream cheese; beat with a mixer until smooth. Add remaining ingredients. Pour the mixture into an oiled 4-cup mold and chill several hours or overnight. Unmold and garnish with parsley. Serve with crackers. Serves 12.

SPINACH COCKTAIL BALLS

One of my favorites

2 (10 ounce) packages frozen chopped spinach, cooked and drained *well*
2 cups prepared stuffing mix
2 medium size onions, grated
6 eggs, beaten
¾ cup butter or margarine, melted
½ cup Parmesan cheese, grated (fresh is best)
1 teaspoon garlic salt
1 teaspoon black pepper
½ teaspoon thyme

Preheat oven to 350 degrees. Mix ingredients together and form into bite size balls. Freeze on a cookie sheet; then store in freezer in plastic bags. Thaw 10 minutes before using. Bake 15 to 20 minutes. Serve hot. Makes 60 to 70.

Rita Drummond
Columbus, North Carolina

SPRINGTIME FILLING FOR COCKTAIL SANDWICHES

Unusual and delicious

- 2 tomatoes, peeled and seeded
- 1 cucumber, peeled and seeded (cut in half lengthwise; scoop out seeds)
- 1 green pepper, finely chopped
- 1 onion, finely chopped
- 1 cup celery, finely chopped
- 2 teaspoons salt
- 1 envelope unflavored gelatin
- 2 cups mayonnaise
- 3 medium size loaves very thinly sliced bread (very fresh), crust removed and cut in half

Make the day before serving. Combine all vegetables and chop fine. Place in colander over a bowl in which gelatin has been sprinkled. Sprinkle vegetables with salt and let stand 1 hour or more. This allows juice to drip into the gelatin. Heat juice and gelatin; remove from heat and add mayonnaise. Add vegetables and blend. Keep refrigerated in tightly covered jar. When ready to prepare, spread vegetable filling on one slice of bread; cover with another slice. Will keep for a week. Serves 20.

Leila Stringer
Anderson, South Carolina

PEANUT BUTTER FINGERS

Good with coffee, tea or cocktails

1 large loaf of sandwich bread, frozen
1 (13 ounce) jar smooth peanut butter
½ cup vegetable oil
2 tablespoons sugar

Preheat oven to 250 degrees. Remove crusts from bread and cut each slice into 8 pieces. Bake sticks and crusts in oven until light brown, 45 minutes to 1 hour. Crush crusts in a baggie with rolling pin (or use a can of unseasoned bread crumbs). Place on cookie sheet with sides. Heat peanut butter, oil and sugar in the top of a double boiler. Mix well. Dip bread sticks, a few at a time, into mixture. Roll peanut butter sticks in crumbs. Stack log fashion to dry. These freeze well. Makes over 100 sticks.

WILHELMINA'S SMOKED SALMON BALL

Good flavor

1 (16 ounce) can red salmon
1 (8 ounce) package cream cheese, softened
1 tablespoon fresh lemon juice
2 teaspoons finely grated onion
1 teaspoon prepared horseradish
¼ teaspoon salt
¼ teaspoon liquid smoke
½ cup pecans, chopped
3 tablespoons chopped fresh parsley

Drain and flake salmon; combine with cream cheese, lemon juice, onion, horseradish, salt and liquid smoke. Chill several hours. Combine pecans and parsley. Shape salmon mixture into one large ball or two small ones. Roll in nut mixture. Chill again. Serve with crackers. May be frozen. Serves 12.

Wilhelmina
Quincy, Illinois

CHICKEN NUGGETS

A wonderful appetizer that should win a prize

4 whole large chicken breasts, skinned, boned
Beau Monde seasoning
½ cup butter, melted
1 cup seasoned bread crumbs
½ teaspoon onion powder
¼ teaspoon salt
Dash pepper
¼ cup grated Parmesan cheese

Preheat oven to 375 degrees. Cut chicken into pieces the size of a walnut. Shake Beau Monde seasoning over the pieces. Dip chicken in butter. Mix crumbs with onion powder, salt, pepper and Parmesan cheese. Dip each chicken piece into crumb mixture. Arrange on a cookie sheet and bake 15 to 20 minutes, or until nicely browned. Yield: 40 pieces.

Marian Logan
St. Louis, Missouri

CHERRIES THAT BOUNCE

"This recipe is a version of the traditional Louisiana Cherry Bounce, which is made with wild cherries and any ole white lightnin'—Enjoy it"

1 quart maraschino cherries with stems
1½ cups bourbon, about

Pour off and discard one-half the cherry liquid. Fill jar to top with bourbon. You now have a full quart of cherries in a liquor of half maraschino juice and half bourbon. Allow to age at least three weeks. Drink the bounce happily, and then serve the cherries as a cocktail nibble. Will keep a year or more at room temperature, but the cherries keep getting heftier and heftier.

Pat Baldridge
Food Editor, *State-Times* and *Morning Advocate*
Baton Rouge, Louisiana

Courtesy of Dottie Neville
Jupiter, Florida

CHERRY CORDIALS

20-24 Cherries That Bounce
¾ cup real semi-sweet chocolate morsels

Drain and freeze cherries. Melt chocolate in top of a double boiler over low heat. When cherries are frozen, dry on a paper towel and quickly dip, one at a time, into chocolate, swirling around by the stem until completely coated. Place cherries on a rack which is covered with wax paper; refrigerate. Cordials may be frozen.

TUNA FISH HORS D'OEUVRE MOLD

Lovely for a bridge luncheon too

1 envelope unflavored gelatin
¼ cup cold water
2 (6½ to 7 ounce) cans white meat of tuna, drained
2 cups Hellmann's mayonnaise
2 hard-cooked eggs, chopped
½ cup stuffed green olives, chopped
2 tablespoons capers

Dissolve gelatin in cold water to soften. Place over very low heat, stirring constantly, until dissolved. Combine tuna fish, mayonnaise, eggs, olives and capers. Add dissolved gelatin and mix. Pour into an oiled 5½-cup fish mold. Chill in refrigerator overnight or until firm. Unmold onto a serving platter and garnish with watercress or parsley. Decorate mold with sliced stuffed olives and pimento strips for nose, eyes, mouth and fins, if you wish. As a salad, for luncheon, garnish with avocado slices, peeled tomato wedges and Bibb lettuce. Serves 15 to 20 as an hors d'oeuvre and 6 to 8 as a salad.

Caroline Hicks
Opelika, Alabama

CHEESE SURPRISES

These are popular—and for a very good reason

2 cups sharp Cheddar cheese, grated
½ cup butter, softened
2 cups flour, sifted
5 or 6 dashes cayenne
4 tablespoons dry sherry
Large jar tiny stuffed Spanish olives, drained

Preheat oven to 400 degrees. Allow cheese to soften to room temperature. Cream together cheese and butter. Add flour, cayenne and sherry. Mix well, by hand, until pieces of cheese disappear and mixture is smooth. Place a small amount of dough in the palm of the hand and flatten to the size of a silver dollar. Put well-drained olive in center, wrap dough around it and roll into a ball. Place on a cookie sheet and put in the freezer. When frozen, place in plastic bags and seal. To serve, bake frozen on ungreased cookie sheet about 20 minutes, or until lightly browned. Serve hot. Makes 8 or 9 dozen.

Evelyn Searles
Harbor Springs, Michigan

CHEESE ROUNDS

Very crisp and a nice flavor

8 ounces very sharp Cheddar, finely shredded
½ cup butter, softened
¼ teaspoon salt
8 drops Tabasco
1 cup flour

Preheat oven to 400 degrees. Blend cheese and butter until thoroughly mixed and smooth; add salt and Tabasco. Add flour, blend until well mixed. Chill dough. Divide dough into three parts. Roll each between hands until about 1 inch in diameter. Roll in wax paper and chill again. Slice ⅛ inch thick. Bake on slightly buttered sheet 7 to 8 minutes. Watch carefully so they do not get too brown. Remove from sheet immediately. May freeze. Makes 120 rounds.

Ina Edens
Tryon, North Carolina

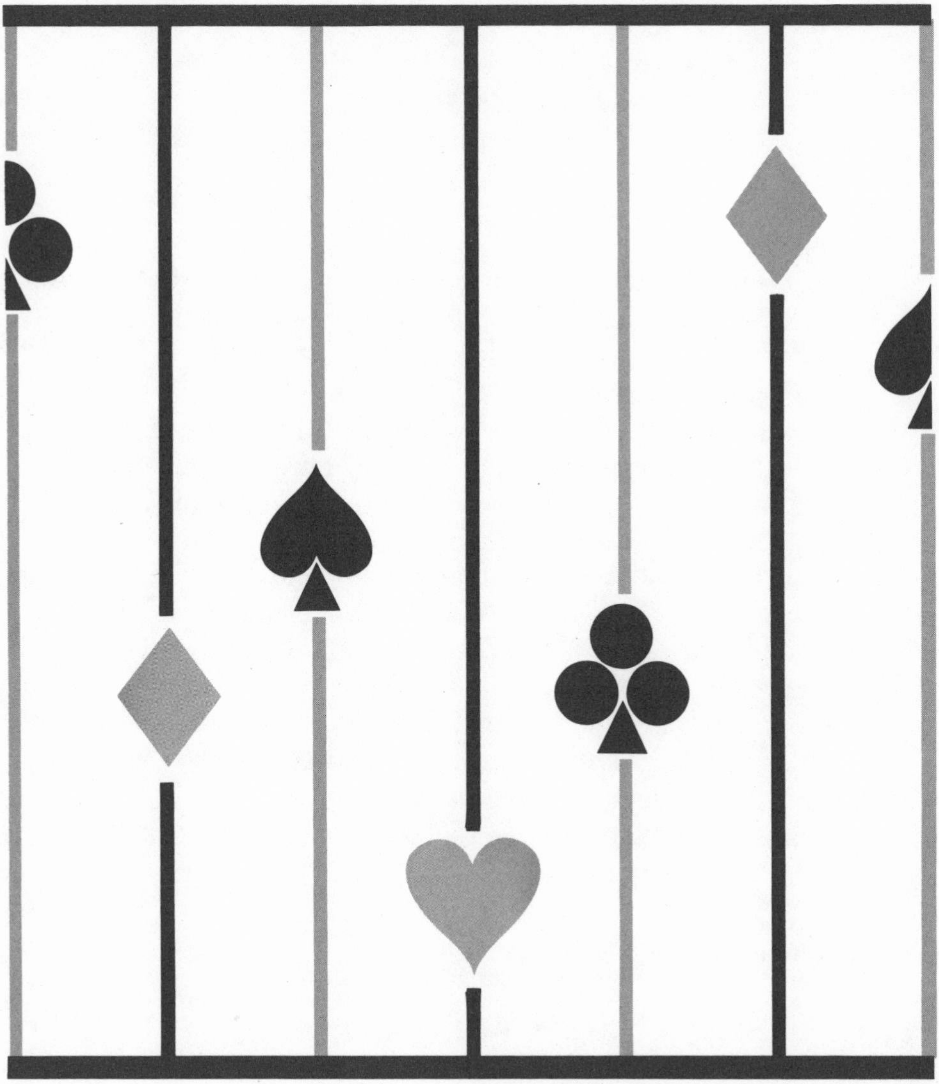

SOUPS and SALADS

APPLE CURRY SOUP

Fabulous

2 medium onions, thinly sliced
2 tablespoons butter
6 red apples, peeled and diced
2 tablespoons sugar (dependent upon sweetness of apples and taste)
4 cups chicken broth
1 tablespoon curry powder (2 tablespoons if stronger curry flavor is desired)
Salt and white pepper to taste
1 to 2 pints light cream
Finely chopped parsley
Toasted slivered almonds

In a large deep skillet sauté onions in butter until transparent. Add apples, sugar, if needed, and broth. Cook over low heat until apples are soft. Mix a small amount of broth with curry powder, salt and pepper; blend. Stir into remaining broth; taste and adjust seasonings. Purée in food processor or blender, adding cream according to desired richness and consistency; do not let it be too thin. Refrigerate. Serve very cold. Sprinkle parsley and toasted almonds on top. Freezes well. Serves 8.

Peggy Carr
Les Cheneaux Club, Cedarville, Michigan

MOCK VICHYSSOISE

It is delicious!!!

2 (10¾ ounce) cans cream of potato soup
2 (14½ ounce) cans chicken broth
2 (8 ounce) cartons sour cream
2 teaspoons grated onion
Chopped chives for garnish

Place soups, sour cream and onion in a blender or mixing bowl. Beat until thoroughly combined and smooth. Chill for several hours. Garnish generously with chopped chives. Serve very cold. Serves 8 to 10.

Alta Savage
Vero Beach, Florida

GARDEN SOUP CHILLED

I pleaded for this one . . . you'll be glad I did

2 tablespoons butter
1 cup chopped green onions with tops
1 cup thinly sliced potato
3 cups chicken broth
1 teaspoon dill weed
1 large cucumber, chopped
2 cups shredded lettuce
Salt and freshly ground pepper, to taste
1 cup yogurt

Melt butter in a large pan. Add onions and potato and sauté over low heat for 10 minutes. Stir in the broth, dill weed, cucumber, lettuce, salt and pepper. Heat to boiling, reduce heat and simmer 15 to 20 minutes. Cool. Add yogurt and stir. Put half of the mixture at a time in blender and whip at high speed until smooth, about 30 seconds. Chill for several hours in the refrigerator. Garnish with chives, if desired. Serves 6.

Barbara Eitel
Vero Beach, Florida

TOMATO BISQUE

Serve piping hot in mugs and pass an appetizer tray

3 cups canned tomatoes
1 tablespoon finely grated onion
¼ teaspoon celery seed
2 whole cloves
1 bay leaf
¼ cup butter
¼ cup flour
1 quart milk
½ cup Roquefort or bleu cheese
Salt and pepper to taste
Parsley for garnish

In a saucepan combine tomatoes, onion, celery seed, cloves and bay leaf. Cover and simmer gently for 15 minutes. Strain through a fine sieve. Melt butter in a saucepan, add flour, blend and stir for 2 minutes to eliminate raw flour taste. Add milk, stirring constantly until sauce is smooth and thickened. Add cheese and stir until melted. Continue stirring, gradually adding hot tomato mixture. Season with salt and pepper and heat to serving temperature. Serves 6.

LOU'S COLD AVOCADO SOUP

Company special for a hot day

1 medium size onion, grated
1 stalk celery, minced
2 tablespoons butter
1 tablespoon flour
2 teaspoons curry
1 firm, tart apple, peeled and chopped
4 cups chicken broth
2 medium size avocados, peeled and chopped
1 cup cream or half and half
¼ teaspoon salt
Dash white pepper
Pinch sugar
3 to 4 dashes Tabasco
Thin slices avocado
Very thin slices apple

Sauté onion and celery, on very low heat, in butter until clear. Stir in flour and curry; cook, stirring constantly, until blended. Add chopped apple and half of the chicken broth. Stir and cook until apples are soft. Transfer to blender, and add avocado and purée. Return to saucepan; add remaining chicken broth, cream, salt, pepper, sugar and Tabasco. Mix well. Serve very cold. Garnish with a thin slice of avocado and a very thin slice of apple. Serves 6 to 8.

Lou Steffens
Salisbury, Maryland

GAZPACHO

An elegant first course

2 cups canned tomato purée
1 onion, chopped
1 green pepper, chopped
1 cucumber, peeled and chopped
2 cups tomato juice
1 tablespoon olive oil
3 tablespoons cider vinegar
1 clove garlic, crushed
1 teaspoon salt
½ teaspoon ground cumin

Blend purée and vegetables on chop control in blender for 30 seconds. Pour juice, olive oil, vinegar and seasonings into a large bowl. Mix together. Stir in tomato mixture. Chill for several hours. Serve in bouillon cups. Serves 8.

Henrietta Heaviside
Skaneateles, New York

CRAB BISQUE

Superb for your bridge foursome

1 (11¼ ounce) can cream of green pea soup
1 (10¾ ounce) can cream of tomato soup
1½ cups half and half cream, heated
1 cup fresh crabmeat
Salt and pepper to taste
1 tablespoon dry sherry in each soup bowl
Chopped parsley for garnish

Combine the soups and heat to the boiling point. Over low heat, stir in heated cream. Flake the crabmeat, add salt and pepper and combine with soup. When hot, pour over sherry in soup bowls. Garnish with parsley. Serves 4.

Laura Nichols
Evanston, Illinois

ARTICHOKES IN ASPIC

1 (1 pound) can artichoke hearts, cut in thirds
8 seedless ripe olives, cut in halves
2 envelopes unflavored gelatin
3½ cups canned tomato-vegetable juice
2 teaspoons Worcestershire sauce
2 tablespoons lemon juice
1 tablespoon horseradish
1 teaspoon salt (scant)
2 to 3 dashes Tabasco

Drain artichoke hearts; add olives; set aside. Dissolve gelatin in ½ cup vegetable juice. Heat remaining 3 cups juice to boiling. Add gelatin; stir until dissolved. Add the seasonings. Pour a small smount of gelatin mixture in the bottom of a 6-cup mold. Chill until firm. Arrange artichoke hearts and olives on top of firm mixture. Pour remaining mixture on top; refrigerate until firm. Unmold on salad greens and serve with mayonnaise. Serves 8.

SPINACH SALAD

Extra good

½ pound bacon
½ cup sugar
1½ tablespoons bacon drippings
½ cup vinegar
¾ teaspoon salt
1 egg, beaten
1 pound fresh spinach
5 small scallions, chopped fine

Fry bacon in a skillet over moderately high heat until crisp and brown. Drain on paper towel. Crumble. Reserve 1½ tablespoons bacon drippings. Set aside. Combine sugar, bacon drippings, vinegar, salt and egg in a small pan. Cook over medium low heat, stirring constantly, until slightly thickened. Refrigerate. Wash and thoroughly dry spinach; break leaves into bite-size pieces. When ready to serve, add chopped scallions, crumbled bacon; pour cold dressing over all and toss lightly until leaves are coated. Serves 4.

Jane Todd
Vero Beach, Florida

CRANBERRY SALAD AND RAW CRANBERRY RELISH

Deserves a blue ribbon

1 package unflavored gelatin
¼ cup cold water
1¾ cups boiling water
1 teaspoon sugar
1½ cups raw cranberry relish
½ cup pecans, chopped

Dissolve gelatin in cold water. Add boiling water to gelatin mixture. Stir until blended. Cool. Add sugar, cranberry relish and pecans. Pour into 6 individual molds. Refrigerate until firm. Serves 6.

Raw Cranberry Relish:

A wonderful accompaniment for meat

4 cups cranberries
2 Delicious apples
Orange peel of ½ an orange
2 large oranges
2 cups sugar

Put cranberries, apples and orange peel through a food processor (coarse blade). Cut orange sections into small pieces; add to cranberry mixture. Add sugar; mix well. Refrigerate. This will keep for days in the refrigerator and freezes well for months and months. Makes 5½ cups.

Purefoy Hotel
Talladega, Alabama

Courtesy of Elizabeth Salter
Auburn, Alabama

FRESH PEAR SALAD

Pretty and good

Halve and core ripe fresh pears. Soften Philadelphia cream cheese with mayonnaise to make soft enough to spread. Place pear, cut side down, on bread board and cover the outside surface with softened cheese. Stud it with halved seedless grapes all over the cheese, pressing the cut side of the grapes well into the cheese. Place on nest of Bibb lettuce and serve with chutney French dressing. To make chutney dressing, add ¼ cup finely chopped chutney to ½ cup French dressing.

MOLDED SALMON SALAD WITH CUCUMBER DRESSING

1 (10¾ ounce) can tomato soup
1 (8 ounce) package cream cheese, softened
2 tablespoons unflavored gelatin
½ cup cold water
1 (1 pound) can salmon
1 green pepper, chopped fine
1 small onion, grated
1 cup celery, cut fine
1 cup mayonnaise

Heat soup in the top of a double boiler. Add cream cheese and stir until melted. Dissolve gelatin in cold water and add to soup mixture. Remove from heat; add salmon, pepper, onion, celery and mayonnaise. Mix well. Put in an oiled fish mold and chill several hours.

Cucumber Dressing:

½ cup whipping cream, whipped
1 cup mayonnaise
2 tablespoons lemon juice
¼ teaspoon salt
⅛ teaspoon white pepper
1 small cucumber, well drained, chopped fine

Fold whipped cream into mayonnaise; stir in lemon juice. Add salt, pepper and well-drained cucumber. Chill. Serve separately with the salmon mold. Serves 8.

EMERALD PARTY SALAD

Beautiful and delicious

4 (3 ounce) packages lime flavored Jello
7 cups boiling water
1 cup diced pineapple
1 cup slivered almonds
1 pint sour cream

Dissolve gelatin in boiling water. Jell slightly. Add pineapple, almonds and sour cream. Pour into 18 to 20 individual molds. Refrigerate until firm.

Dressing:

2 tablespoons butter
2 tablespoons flour, sifted
½ cup sugar (skimpy)
2 egg yolks
1¼ cups warm pineapple juice
⅛ teaspoon salt
2 egg whites
2 tablespoons sugar
1 cup whipping cream, whipped

In the top of a double boiler, melt butter, add flour; mix until smooth and stir 3 to 4 minutes. Add sugar, egg yolks mixed with ¼ cup pineapple juice and salt. Stir. Add remaining cup pineapple juice. Stir constantly until mixture is thick; simmer a few more minutes. Cool. Beat until just blended, 2 egg whites with sugar; add to pineapple juice mixture. Fold in whipped cream. Refrigerate. Serves 18 to 20.

EXOTIC CHICKEN SALAD

An immediate family favorite

3 cups cooked chicken, cut in chunks
1 cup baked ham, cut in chunks
1 (8 ounce) can sliced water chestnuts
2 cups seedless green grapes
1 cup celery, chopped
1 cup sliced almonds, toasted (save ¼ cup for garnish)
1 cup mayonnaise
½ cup sour cream
2 teaspoons curry powder
1 teaspoon soy sauce
4 tablespoons lemon juice
1 (13 ounce) can chunk pineapple, drained

Combine first six ingredients. Mix mayonnaise, sour cream, curry powder, soy sauce and lemon juice; blend well. Toss mayonnaise mixture with chicken and chill several hours. To serve spoon on Bibb lettuce and sprinkle with pineapple chunks and remaining toasted almonds. Serves 8.

Helen Warren
Vero Beach, Florida

FROZEN STRAWBERRY SALAD

A delicious salad for a ladies luncheon

1 cup whipping cream, whipped
2 (3 ounce) packages cream cheese, softened
1 cup Hellmann's mayonnaise
16 large marshmallows, cut fine
1 (16 ounce) package frozen strawberries, partially thawed and drained
1 (1 pound, 4 ounce) can crushed pineapple, drained
1 cup pecans, chopped

Fold the whipping cream into softened cream cheese. Add mayonnaise, marshmallows, strawberries, pineapple and pecans. Stir gently to mix. Freeze in oiled molds or 2½ quart oblong pyrex dish. Serves 10 to 12.

Trudy Jackson
Opelika, Alabama

ORANGE-APRICOT RING

Really lovely!

2 (1 pound) cans apricot halves
2 (3 ounce) packages orange flavored gelatin
Dash salt
1 (6 ounce) can frozen orange juice
2 tablespoons lemon juice
1 (7 ounce) bottle lemon-lime carbonated beverage

Drain apricots, reserving 1½ cups syrup. Purée apricots in blender or put through a sieve. Combine reserved syrup, gelatin, salt and heat to boiling, stirring to dissolve gelatin. Remove from heat. Add apricot purée, orange juice concentrate and lemon juice to gelatin mixture and stir to melt concentrate. Slowly pour lemon-lime beverage down side of pan. To keep bubbles, mix gently with an up and down motion. Pour into 6½-cup ring mold. Chill until firm, about 6 hours or overnight. Serves 10 to 12.

Ina Edens
Tryon, North Carolina

THREE-DAY-AHEAD COLE SLAW

Perfect for the barbecue crowd

1 medium size head of cabbage, shredded
1 medium size onion, minced
1 green pepper, chopped fine
1 (4 ounce) jar pimento, chopped fine

Dressing:

½ cup honey
½ cup vinegar
½ cup oil
2 teaspoons sugar
2 teaspoons salt
½ teaspoon mustard seed
Dash pepper

Place cabbage, onion, pepper and pimento in a large bowl; mix. Put all ingredients for dressing in saucepan. Bring to a boil. Immediately pour over cabbage mixture and refrigerate, covered. Stir occasionally and serve three days later. Keeps well for at least a week. Serves 8.

Barbara Eitel
Vero Beach, Florida

HOT CHICKEN SALAD

Good for a bridge luncheon or any time

2 cups cooked chicken
1 cup mayonnaise
2 tablespoons lemon juice
2 cups thinly sliced celery
2 teaspoons grated onion
½ teaspoon salt
Few dashes cayenne pepper
½ cup chopped toasted almonds
½ cup grated sharp Cheddar cheese
1 cup finely crushed fresh potato chips

Preheat oven to 425 degrees. Combine all ingredients but cheese and potato chips. Mix well. Place in a 2 quart buttered baking dish. Sprinkle with cheese and top with potato chips. Bake about 15 minutes. Serves 4 to 6.

Dottie Neville
Jupiter, Florida

SOUR CREAM POTATO SALAD

There is none better

5 cups diced, boiled potatoes
1 tablespoon grated onion
½ cup diced cucumber
¾ teaspoon celery seed
1½ teaspoons salt
½ teaspoon freshly ground pepper
1 tablespoon chopped parsley
3 hard-cooked eggs, whites diced, yolks mashed
1½ cups sour cream
½ cup Hellmann's mayonnaise
¼ cup vinegar
1 teaspoon prepared mustard

Potato salad is best made from red waxy potatoes, cooked in their jackets and peeled and marinated while still warm. Combine potatoes, onion, cucumber, celery seed, salt, pepper and parsley and mix together lightly. Add diced whites to potato mixture. Combine mashed yolks with sour cream, mayonnaise, vinegar and mustard; add to potatoes and gently blend together. Refrigerate several hours. Taste; some like a little more salt and pepper. Serves 10.

CALICO BEAN SALAD

Wonderful for a buffet supper

1 (16 ounce) can red kidney beans
1 (16 ounce) can French-cut green beans
1 (16 ounce) can yellow wax beans
½ cup onion, minced
½ cup green pepper, minced
½ cup salad oil
½ cup cider vinegar
¾ cup sugar
1 teaspoon salt
½ teaspoon pepper

Drain beans and place in a glass bowl. Add onions and green pepper. Mix oil and vinegar with sugar, salt and pepper. Pour over bean mixture. Blend thoroughly. Cover and refrigerate several hours. Serves 10.

GRAPE AND WINE SALAD

A beautiful ring mold and delicious too

¾ cup sugar
2½ envelopes unflavored gelatin
1 cup water
2 cups white wine
¾ cup sweet sherry
4 cups seedless green grapes (about 1½ pounds)
Juice of 1 lemon

In the top of a double boiler mix sugar and gelatin. Add water and stir over low heat until dissolved. Remove from heat; add white wine, sherry, grapes and lemon juice. Pour into a 6-cup ring mold and refrigerate until firm. Serve with the following sauce:

Sauce #1:

¾ cup half and half cream
3 egg yolks
2 tablespoons sugar
1 teaspoon vanilla
⅔ cup heavy cream, whipped

Put cream in the top of a double boiler. With a hand beater, beat until it bubbles. Add yolks and sugar. Over low heat, cook until it thickens (like custard), stirring constantly . . . about 15 minutes. Cool. Add vanilla and fold in whipped cream.

Sauce #2:
Easier! and good

1 cup heavy cream, whipped
1 cup mayonnaise
1 mashed banana (optional)

Fold the mayonnaise into the whipped cream. Serves 12.

Leila Stringer
Anderson, South Carolina

TOMATOES LUTECE

The restacking is different and attractive.
The marinade is delicious

8 firm ripe tomatoes
1 clove garlic, crushed
1 teaspoon salt
1 teaspoon sugar
¼ teaspoon black pepper
¼ cup olive oil
2 tablespoons tarragon or cider vinegar
2 tablespoons prepared mustard (Dijon type)
¼ cup chopped parsley

Peel and slice tomatoes crosswise into ¼ inch thick slices. Restack and place in a shallow serving dish. Combine all ingredients but parsley in a small jar. Cover and shake well. Pour over tomatoes. Cover lightly and refrigerate. Let stand at room temperature for 20 minutes before serving. Sprinkle parsley over tomatoes as dish is being assembled. Serves 8.

Carol Porter
Lake Zurich, Illinois

CELERY SEED DRESSING

Wonderful on avocado and grapefruit, Bibb lettuce or any fruit

½ cup sugar
1 teaspoon dry mustard
1 teaspoon salt
⅓ cup vinegar
1 cup vegetable oil
1 tablespoon celery seed
¼ cup onion, finely grated

Mix sugar, dry mustard, salt and vinegar. Add oil gradually, and beat with electric beater until well blended. Add celery seed and onion; mix well. Refrigerate. This will keep for 1 month in refrigerator. Makes 1½ cups.

Elizabeth Salter
Auburn, Alabama

BLENDER MAYONNAISE

Lovely flavor, takes two minutes

1 cup salad oil
1 egg plus 1 yolk
2 tablespoons fresh lemon juice
1 tablespoon finely grated onion
½ teaspoon salt
½ teaspoon dry mustard

Before making, have oil, egg and lemon juice chilled. Combine ¼ cup salad oil with all remaining ingredients in blender. Blend on low speed for 4 to 5 seconds. Add remaining oil and blend about 45 seconds more, until thick.

Beverly Wood
Vero Beach, Florida

WATERCRESS SALAD DRESSING

1 bunch watercress, tops only
1 bunch parsley, tops only
8 small shallots, minced
⅓ cup vinegar
1 cup safflower oil
3 egg yolks
½ teaspoon Aćcent
½ teaspoon horseradish
1 teaspoon Vege-Sal seasoned salt (available at health food stores)
¼ teaspoon Worcestershire sauce
Pinch of dry mustard, or to taste

Blend all ingredients in blender. If dressing is too thick, thin with ice water, adding a very small amount at a time. Makes 2½ cups.

Peggy Fulenwider
Denver, Colorado

MEXICAN VILLAGE SALAD DRESSING

1 quart safflower oil
5 tablespoons lemon juice
4 cloves garlic
1 tablespoon peppercorns
4 ounces Roquefort cheese
1 tablespoon salt
½ teaspoon dry mustard
Dash of Accent

Place all ingredients in blender and blend well. Cover and refrigerate. Age for three weeks. Keeps indefinitely.

Margie Wood
Grosse Pointe, Michigan

SPECIAL SEA FOOD DRESSING

Perfect with shrimp or crabmeat

1½ cups Hellmann's mayonnaise
2 teaspoons onion, finely grated
1 teaspoon Worcestershire sauce
2 tablespoons lemon juice
2 tablespoons finely chopped green pepper (optional)

Mix all ingredients thoroughly. Refrigerate. Serves 6.

Cherry Sue Jackson
Opelika, Alabama

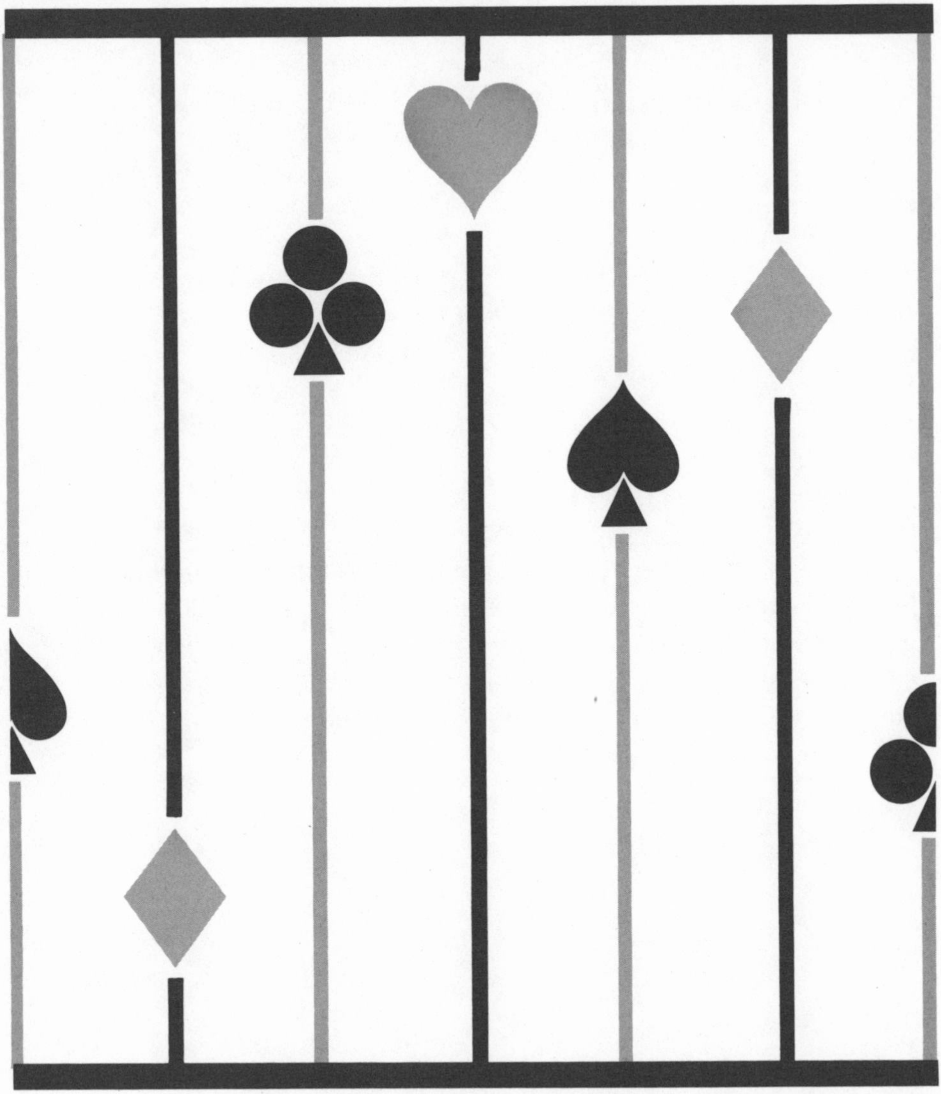

MAIN COURSES

CHICKEN AND ARTICHOKE CASSEROLE

An excellent combination

6 whole chicken breasts, boned, split and skinned
Paprika
Salt
Pepper
1 cup butter
2 (15 ounce) cans artichoke hearts
1 pound fresh mushrooms
¼ teaspoon tarragon
6 tablespoons flour
1 cup dry sherry
3 cups chicken bouillon

Preheat oven to 350 degrees. Coat chicken breast with paprika, salt and pepper. Sauté chicken in ½ cup of the butter until brown; remove. Place in a casserole and add artichoke hearts. Put mushrooms and remaining butter in skillet, season with tarragon and sauté 5 minutes. Sprinkle in flour; add sherry and bouillon. Simmer 5 minutes and pour over chicken and artichokes. Cover casserole and bake 45 minutes. Serves 8.

Elizabeth Lafferty
Hollidaysburg, Pennsylvania

ELEGANT CHICKEN

It is!

3 large chicken breasts, boned and skinned
½ cup all-purpose flour
2 teaspoons salt
2 teaspoons paprika
½ cup milk
4 cups hot, cooked rice
Lemon cream sauce

Cut chicken breasts into ½ inch strips. Combine flour, salt and paprika. Dip chicken strips into milk, then roll in seasoned flour. Heat fat ½ inch deep in skillet. Add chicken strips and fry until golden brown. To serve, mound rice on serving dish, top with lemon cream sauce and fried chicken strips.

Lemon Cream Sauce:

¼ cup butter
¼ cup all-purpose flour
1 teaspoon salt
¼ teaspoon paprika
2 chicken bouillon cubes
1½ cups water
1 cup heavy cream
2 teaspoons lemon juice

Melt butter in saucepan. Blend in flour, salt, paprika and cut-up bouillon cubes. Gradually add water and cook, stirring constantly, until mixture thickens and comes to a boil. Add cream and heat to serving temperature. Stir in lemon juice. Serves 6.

CHICKEN BREASTS WITH ORANGE SAUCE

A gourmet's delight

3 large chicken breasts, boned, split and skinned
1 teaspoon salt
¼ cup butter
2 tablespoons flour
2 tablespoons sugar
¼ teaspoon dry mustard
¼ teaspoon cinnamon
⅛ teaspoon ginger
1½ cups orange juice

Sprinkle chicken breasts with ½ teaspoon of the salt. Melt butter in a large skillet. Add chicken and brown both sides. Remove from skillet. Add flour, sugar, mustard, cinnamon, ginger and remaining ½ teaspoon salt to drippings in pan. Stir to a smooth paste. Gradually add orange juice and cook, stirring constantly, until mixture thickens and comes to a boil. Add chicken breasts. Cover; simmer over low heat until chicken is tender, about 25 to 30 minutes. If you wish, 3 cups of hot cooked rice may be served with the chicken. May be done ahead. Reheats well. Serves 4 to 6.

Evelyn Searles
Harbor Springs, Michigan

CREAMED CHICKEN

A particularly good recipe

2 tablespoons butter
3 tablespoons flour
1 cup chicken broth
⅓ cup heavy cream
2 cups cubed cooked breast of chicken
Salt and white pepper to taste
2 tablespoons chopped parsley
1 teaspoon dry sherry (optional)
Watercress, paprika for garnish

In the top of a double boiler melt butter; add flour and stir for 2 to 3 minutes to eliminate raw flour taste. Slowly add chicken broth, stirring constantly until thickened. Add heavy cream, chicken, salt and pepper, parsley and sherry. Cook over low heat for 20 to 30 minutes so the chicken will absorb some of the sauce and be moist. Serve on toast, waffle, patty shell or with rice. Garnish. Serves 4.

CHICKEN DIABLE

So easy and so good

1 broiler-fryer cut up or 3 breasts, split
¼ cup butter
½ cup honey
¼ cup prepared mustard
1 teaspoon salt
1 teaspoon curry

Preheat oven to 375 degrees. Wash and dry chicken. Remove skin. Melt butter in shallow baking pan. Stir into butter the honey, mustard, salt and curry. Roll chicken into butter mixture, coating both sides. Arrange meaty side up in single layer in baking pan. Bake 1 hour, or until chicken is tender and richly glazed. Serves 4.

Betty Dragoo
Vero Beach, Florida

CHEESE SOUFFLÉ

Everyone loves this!

¼ cup butter
¼ cup flour
1 cup milk
½ teaspoon salt
¾ cup shredded sharp Cheddar cheese
4 egg yolks, beaten
4 egg whites, beaten stiff
2 tablespoons Parmesan cheese
4 (10 ounce) individual buttered casseroles

Preheat oven to 375 degrees. Melt butter; blend in flour and cook 2 to 3 minutes to remove raw flour taste. Heat milk and add slowly to butter-flour mixture. Add salt. Cook until thick; add cheese and stir until cheese is melted. Remove from heat and stir in egg yolks. Cool. Fold in beaten egg whites. Spoon into 4 casserole dishes, sprinkle with Parmesan cheese. Bake in a pan of water 25 to 30 minutes.

Served every Monday to the bridge players at the Woman's Athletic Club of Chicago.
This recipe is included by special permission of the club.

FAMOUS WELSH RAREBIT

Good! It's the beer that does it!

1 tablespoon butter
1 cup beer
1 pound sharp Cheddar cheese, shredded
1 egg, slightly beaten
¼ teaspoon dry mustard
1 teaspoon salt
1 teaspoon Worcestershire sauce
Few dashes cayenne pepper
Few dashes paprika

Melt butter in the top of a double boiler. Stir in beer. When beer is warm, add cheese; stir constantly, over low heat, with a fork until cheese is melted. Stir in slightly beaten egg. Combine mustard, salt, Worcestershire sauce and stir into cheese. When very smooth, add cayenne and paprika. Serve at once on crisp hot toast. Suggested accompaniment: Broiled tomato halves. Serves 6.

BREAKFAST STRATA

I love things that can be made the day before!
A fine way to start the day

1 pound hot sausage
6 eggs
2 cups milk
½ teaspoon salt
1 teaspoon dry mustard
4 slices bread, cubed, lightly buttered
1½ cups shredded sharp Cheddar cheese

Cook sausage until done, breaking it into small pieces while cooking. Drain well; set aside. Beat eggs, add milk, salt, mustard; blend well. Butter an 8 inch square baking pan. Layer bread, sausage and cheese. Pour egg mixture over these ingredients. Cover; refrigerate overnight. Bake in a preheated 350 degree oven for 30 minutes. Serves 8.

Phyl Miller
Blowing Rock, North Carolina

CHEESE PUDDING

Guests always want the recipe

5 slices bread, buttered
¾ pound sharp Cheddar cheese, shredded
4 eggs, beaten slightly
2 cups milk
½ teaspoon dry mustard
½ teaspoon salt
Pinch cayenne pepper

Tear or tuft bread into small pieces and add cheese. Place in the bottom of a 2-quart casserole. Mix the egg, milk and seasonings together. Pour over the bread and cheese mixture and push down to cover. Place in refrigerator overnight before cooking. Preheat oven to 350 degrees. Put casserole in a pan of water and bake about an hour. The pudding keeps very well and will not fall if not served immediately. It can be reheated for the next day. To double recipe, double all ingredients but the cheese; use a little more than a pound. Serves 4 to 6.

Barbara Carlson
Glens Falls, New York

CHEESE PIE

Do make this soon! It is special!!

1 (9 inch) deep dish pie crust
1½ cups shredded Monterey Jack cheese
1 cup shredded sharp Cheddar cheese
1 (4 ounce) can green chili peppers, drained, seeded and chopped fine
⅓ cup chopped onions, drain well
⅓ cup chopped tomatoes, drain well
⅓ cup chopped mushrooms
1 cup half and half cream
3 eggs
¼ teaspoon salt
⅛ teaspoon cumin
Dash of Worcestershire sauce

Preheat oven to 400 degrees. Prick the bottom and sides of crust thoroughly with a fork. Bake pie crust for 10 minutes. Remove from oven. Lower oven temperature to 350. Sprinkle all of the Monterey Jack cheese and ½ cup of Cheddar cheese over the bottom of the cooked pie crust. Sprinkle chili peppers over cheeses. Add onions, tomatoes and mushrooms. Pour half and half in blender; add eggs, salt, cumin and Worcestershire. Blend 20 seconds. Pour into pie crust; sprinkle remaining ½ cup Cheddar cheese over filling. Bake 40 to 45 minutes or until tested done with a fork. Let stand 15 minutes before cutting. Serves 6.

Ann McConnell
Toronto, Canada

CURRIED EGGS WITH SHRIMP SAUCE

Excellent for a luncheon

8 hard-cooked eggs
⅓ cup mayonnaise
½ teaspoon salt
½ teaspoon paprika
¼ teaspoon curry powder
¼ teaspoon dry mustard
Shrimp sauce

Preheat oven to 350 degrees. Cut eggs in half lengthwise, remove yolks and mash. Mix with mayonnaise and seasonings. Refill egg whites. Arrange eggs in 8x8-inch buttered baking dish. Top with shrimp sauce.

Shrimp Sauce:

2 tablespoons butter
2 tablespoons flour
1 (10¾ ounce) can frozen shrimp soup
1 soup can milk
½ cup shredded sharp Cheddar cheese
1 cup soft bread crumbs
1 tablespoon melted butter
Parsley for garnish

Melt butter; blend in flour. Stir in soup and milk and cook until sauce thickens. Add cheese, stirring until melted. Cover eggs with sauce. Mix crumbs and melted butter; sprinkle around edge of mixture in baking dish. Bake 15 to 20 minutes or until heated thoroughly. Garnish with parsley. Serves 6 to 8.

Daisy Giles
Lake Forest, Illinois

SHRIMP AND DEVILED EGGS

About the best thing you've ever tasted

8 eggs, deviled
24 large shrimp or 32 medium size, cooked and cleaned
4 tablespoons butter
4 tablespoons flour
¼ teaspoon salt
2 cups half and half or light cream
1 cup shredded sharp Cheddar cheese
Several dashes cayenne pepper
Crushed potato chips

Preheat oven to 350 degrees. In a buttered casserole, or 8 individual casserole dishes, place the deviled eggs and arrange the shrimp around them. Melt butter in a heavy-bottomed pan, blend in flour and salt. Over low heat, stir constantly for 3 or 4 minutes until well blended and the taste of raw flour has vanished. Add the half and half, continue stirring, and cook until mixture thickens. Add cheese and cayenne and cook until cheese melts. Pour over eggs and shrimp. Sprinkle the top with crushed potato chips. Bake for 30 minutes. Serves 8.

Deviled Eggs:

8 hard-cooked eggs
2 tablespoons mayonnaise
2 tablespoons prepared mustard (Dijon type)
¼ teaspoon salt
2 teaspoons vinegar
Several dashes cayenne pepper
¼ teaspoon dry mustard

Cut eggs in half, lengthwise. Remove yolks; put through strainer or mash very well. Add remaining ingredients and blend until smooth. Fill hollow of egg whites. Chill.

Gil True
Vero Beach, Florida

SOLE VÉRONIQUE

6 fillets of sole
Salt and pepper to taste
½ cup white wine
2 tablespoons butter
2 tablespoons flour
1 cup milk
1 cup small white grapes
Minced parsley for garnish

Preheat oven to 350 degrees. Place the fillets in a buttered flat ovenproof serving dish. Add salt and pepper; pour wine over the fillets. Cover the pan with foil and bake 15 minutes. Melt butter; add flour and cook for 3 minutes to remove raw flour taste. Add milk and cook until thick, stirring constantly. Pour off the juice from the fish and add to the cream sauce, mixing well; add half of the grapes to the sauce. Pour the sauce over the fish and place under the broiler just long enough to brown the surface. Place the rest of the grapes around the fillets before serving. Sprinkle with minced parsley. Serves 6.

Marguerite Calhoun
Vero Beach, Florida

SHRIMP ELEGANTÉ

This will delight your bridge foursome

1 (15 ounce) can whole artichoke hearts
¾ pound shrimp, cooked and cleaned
¼ pound fresh mushrooms, sliced
2 tablespoons butter
1½ cups cream sauce
1 tablespoon Worcestershire sauce
¼ cup dry sherry
¼ cup grated Parmesan cheese
Sprinkle of paprika

Preheat oven to 375 degrees. Drain artichoke hearts and arrange them in a buttered shallow baking dish. Spread shrimp over them. Add mushrooms which have been sautéed in butter for about 6 minutes. To cream sauce, add Worcestershire sauce and sherry. After blending well, pour the mixture over the contents of the baking dish. Sprinkle the top with Parmesan cheese and a sprinkling of paprika. Bake for 20 minutes, or until mixture is very hot. Serve from the baking dish. Serves 4.

Cream Sauce:

3 tablespoons butter
3 tablespoons flour
1½ cups half and half cream, scalded
½ teaspoon salt
Dash white pepper

Melt butter in a saucepan over low heat. Stir in flour blending until smooth. Cook, stirring constantly, for 2 to 3 minutes to eliminate the raw flour taste. Gradually add cream; stir until thickened. Add salt and pepper. Makes 1½ cups.

TUNA FLORENTINE STRATA

Another favorite

2 (7 ounce) cans tuna in vegetable oil
⅓ cup chopped scallions
1 (10 ounce) package frozen chopped spinach, thawed and drained
1 cup (4 ounces) shredded Swiss cheese
1 tablespoon lemon juice
1 teaspoon salt, divided
¼ teaspoon dried leaf thyme
6 slices bread, crust removed and cubed
6 eggs
2 cups milk
½ teaspoon dry mustard
⅛ teaspoon cayenne pepper

Preheat oven to 350 degrees. In a large bowl mix tuna, scallions, spinach, Swiss cheese, lemon juice, ¼ teaspoon salt and thyme. Layer half of the bread cubes in a buttered 2-quart soufflé dish, top with half of the tuna mixture, repeat with remaining bread cubes and tuna. Combine eggs, milk, dry mustard, cayenne pepper and remaining ¾ teaspoon salt; pour over tuna. Let stand 2 hours or longer. Place baking dish in a larger pan and add 1 inch of hot water. Bake uncovered for 50 to 60 minutes or until a knife inserted in the center comes out clean. Let stand for 5 minutes. Serves 8.

Jane Stelter
Neenah, Wisconsin

COTELETTES DE SAUMON POJARSKI

(Salmon cutlets with brown butter sauce)
Superb!

1¼ pounds skinless, boneless fillets of fresh salmon (veal or chicken may be substituted)
1½ cups fine fresh bread crumbs
1 cup heavy cream
Salt and freshly ground pepper to taste
¼ teaspoon nutmeg, more or less to taste
Pinch cayenne
4 tablespoons peanut, vegetable or corn oil
8 tablespoons butter

Use the fine blade of a meat grinder and grind the salmon, putting it through once. Do not use a blender. It could be chopped very fine, using a sharp knife. Put the salmon in a mixing bowl and add ½ cup of bread crumbs and ⅓ cup heavy cream, stirring briskly with a wooden spoon. Add salt, pepper, nutmeg and cayenne; continue beating rapidly with the spoon. Beat in the remaining ⅔ cup of heavy cream. Divide the mixture into 6 equal portions; about ¾ of an inch thick. Arrange cutlets on a pan and refrigerate until ready to cook. Coat cutlets on all sides with remaining bread crumbs. Use two skillets. Heat 2 tablespoons oil and 2 tablespoons butter in each skillet and when it is hot, add the salmon cutlets. Cook on one side about 4 minutes, until golden brown, and turn. Cook 3 to 4 minutes longer, until golden brown on the second side. Transfer salmon to a warm platter. Add the remaining 4 tablespoons butter to one of the skillets and cook, shaking the skillet, until the butter starts to brown. Do not let the butter burn. Pour the hot butter over the salmon. Serves 6.

Marilynn B. Alsdorf
Winnetka, Illinois

COMPANY CRABMEAT

Treat your family too

1 pound fresh crabmeat
6 slices good bread, crust removed and cubed
6 tablespoons butter, melted
1 (6 ounce) can water chestnuts, cut up
1 cup mayonnaise
1 cup medium white sauce
2 tablespoons frozen chopped chives
½ cup chopped parsley
1 teaspoon prepared mustard
2 tablespoons lemon juice
½ teaspoon Ac̨cent
3 tablespoons dry sherry
Salt and ground pepper to taste

Preheat oven to 350 degrees. Flake the crabmeat. Sauté bread cubes in butter but do not brown. Set aside. Blend all other ingredients with crabmeat; fold ⅓ of the bread cubes into mixture. Put in a 1½-quart greased casserole and top with remaining bread cubes. Bake for 45 minutes. Can be frozen before baking. Serves 6.

Dorothy Raub
Wilmette, Illinois

LOBSTER FANTAIL

A hostess's dream . . . delicious, easy and make the day before serving

2 (8 ounce) cans lobster meat or
1 (8 ounce) can lobster meat and 1 (8 ounce) can of crabmeat or
2 cans crabmeat or
1 pound fresh crabmeat
1½ cups Swiss cheese, cubed
3 tablespoons green pepper, chopped fine
2 tablespoons onion, grated
½ teaspoon salt
¼ cup mayonnaise
1 teaspoon lemon juice
6 large hamburger rolls (best quality)

Flake lobster or crabmeat. Add cheese, pepper, onion and salt; toss and blend. Mix mayonnaise and lemon juice and add to fish mixture. Slice hamburger rolls twice; butter lightly. Place lobster or crabmeat mixture on each layer. Wrap individually in aluminum foil. Refrigerate. When ready to serve, preheat oven 350 and bake 20 minutes. May freeze. Thaw before baking. Serves 6.

Virginia Soderberg
St. Paul, Minnesota

GRINGO CASSEROLE

Borders on the terrific!

1 medium onion, chopped fine
1 clove garlic, crushed
1 tablespoon vegetable oil
1½ pounds lean ground chuck
1 (8 ounce) can tomato sauce
⅓ cup water
1½ tablespoons chili powder
1 teaspoon oregano
⅛ teaspoon ground cloves
1 (8 ounce) package corn chips

Topping:

2 cups finely shredded lettuce
1 cup shredded sharp Cheddar
Fresh tomatoes, diced

Preheat oven to 325 degrees. Sauté onion and garlic in oil until golden. Add ground chuck and brown. Drain off fat. Add tomato sauce, water, chili powder, oregano and ground cloves. Return to stove over low heat and blend ingredients. Place ½ of the corn chips in a buttered 2-quart baking dish. Spoon half of the meat mixture over chips. Repeat, ending with meat. Bake 20 minutes or until heated thoroughly. Remove from oven and garnish with lettuce, cheese and tomatoes. Serves 6.

MEAT LOAF DIXIE

They love it in California and Connecticut too!

3 pounds ground chuck
1 (1.25 ounce) package onion soup mix
3 eggs, beaten
12 crackers, crushed
1 (16 ounce) can tomatoes, drained, cut up
1 (5.3 ounce) can evaporated milk
3 tablespoons Worcestershire sauce
1 beef bouillon cube
1 cup hot water
1 (10½ ounce) can cream of mushroom soup

Preheat oven to 450 degrees. Combine ground chuck and onion soup mix; blend well with fingers. Add eggs, crackers, tomatoes, milk and Worcestershire sauce and mix well. Make into two loaves and place in two 8½x4½-inch greased pans. Bake until well browned, about 30 minutes. Remove from oven. Add beef bouillon cube to hot water, dissolve completely. Slowly add to mushroom soup and blend well. Pour mushroom soup mixture over the meat loaves, return to oven and bake at 400 for an additional 30 minutes. Baste twice. Serve hot. Serves 8 to 10.

CALIFORNIA BEEF-NOODLE BAKE

A great family dish—guests too!

1 pound ground chuck
½ cup onion, grated
1 tablespoon butter, melted
2 (8 ounce) cans tomato sauce
1 teaspoon sugar
¾ teaspoon salt
¼ teaspoon garlic salt
¼ teaspoon pepper
4 cups uncooked medium noodles
1 cup cream style cottage cheese
1 (8 ounce) package cream cheese, softened
¼ cup sour cream
⅓ cup finely chopped green onions
¼ cup finely chopped green pepper
¼ cup grated Parmesan cheese

Preheat oven to 350 degrees. In a skillet, sauté ground chuck and onion in butter until browned. Stir in tomato sauce, sugar, salt, garlic salt and pepper. Remove from heat. Cook noodles according to package directions; drain. Combine cottage cheese, cream cheese, sour cream, onions and pepper. In a 2 quart casserole, spread half of noodles; top with a little of the meat sauce; cover with cheese mixture; then cover with rest of noodles; add remaining meat sauce. Sprinkle with Parmesan cheese. Bake, uncovered, 30 to 35 minutes, or until hot. May freeze. Serves 8.

Janice Beuttell Cook
Menlo Park, California

THE SENATOR'S FAVORITE PORK CHOPS

Mine Too!

Pork chops
Brown sugar
Chili sauce
2 slices lemon per chop

Preheat oven to 350 degrees. Place pork chops in a baking pan. Put a thick amount of brown sugar on each one. Pour chili sauce on top of sugar; add lemon slices to each chop. Bake, uncovered, for 1 hour.

Sally Danforth
Washington, D. C.

Courtesy of Mettie Dobson
Vero Beach, Florida

PORK À L'ORANGE

Vegetable oil
4 center-cut pork chops
1 (6 ounce) can frozen orange juice concentrate, thawed
6 ounces dry white wine
1 teaspoon dried oregano
1 teaspoon dried sweet basil
Slivered almonds

Preheat oven to 350 degrees. In a heavy skillet heat a small amount of vegetable oil. Add pork chops and fry until nicely browned on both sides. Place in a flat, uncovered baking dish. Set aside. Combine orange juice, wine, oregano and basil. Pour over pork chops. Place in oven and cook for 30 minutes. Sprinkle the top of chops liberally with almonds, spoon the sauce over almonds, and cook 30 minutes longer, or until sauce thickens slightly. Serve with sauce spooned over the chops. Serves 4.

HUNGARIAN GOULASH

Marvelous flavor

2½ pounds sirloin tip beef, cut in 1-inch cubes
2 tablespoons vegetable oil
2 beef bouillon cubes dissolved in 1½ cups boiling water
½ clove garlic, crushed
1 tablespoon Hungarian paprika
5 tablespoons butter or margarine
5 tablespoons flour
¼ cup tomato purée
Wide noodles
Chopped parsley for garnish

Sear beef in vegetable oil. Add bouillon mixture and garlic. Cover and cook over medium heat for 1½ to 2 hours, or until meat is tender. Stir in paprika. Make a paste of butter and flour; stir in a little broth from the beef. Add to the beef mixture to thicken goulash and blend thoroughly. Stir in tomato purée. Serve hot with boiled noodles. Garnish with chopped parsley. Serves 6.

Edith McCarthy
Vero Beach, Florida

CHARLEY'S CHILI

It should win the Championship Chili Cook-Off this year

3 pounds ground chuck, coarsely ground
6 tablespoons vegetable oil
2 cups coarsely chopped onions*, do not pack
2 tablespoons garlic*, finely chopped
4 tablespoons chili powder
1 teaspoon oregano
1 teaspoon ground cumin
1 teaspoon red pepper flakes
4 cups beef stock (I used 5 packets Romanoff MBT Instant Beef Broth)
1 (6 ounce) can tomato paste
1 teaspoon salt
Few grindings black pepper
1 (14 ounce) can dark red kidney beans

In a 12-inch skillet, heat 4 tablespoons of the oil. Add meat and cook over high heat 2 to 3 minutes, until meat is lightly browned. With a slotted spoon transfer to a 4 quart heavy flameproof casserole. Add remaining 2 tablespoons oil to skillet; cook onions and garlic 4 to 5 minutes, stirring frequently. Remove skillet from heat, add chili powder, oregano, cumin and pepper flakes; stir until onions and garlic are well coated. Add to meat. Mix beef stock with tomato paste; blend well; pour over meat mixture in casserole. Add salt and few grindings of pepper. Bring to a boil, stirring once or twice; turn heat to low, half cover pot and simmer 1 to 1½ hours. Add kidney beans 15 minutes before meat is done. Degrease before serving. Serves 6 to 8.

*I called Ohio to check out the amount of onions and garlic! It is true; 2 cups onions and 2 tablespoons garlic. It is excellent chili.

Charles Fairchild
Lakewood, Ohio

LUCY'S SPAGHETTI MEAT SAUCE

None better . . . makes a lot . . . freeze some

3 large onions, chopped
2 cloves garlic, minced
¼ stick butter
¼ cup oil
3 pounds ground chuck
1 pound fresh mushrooms, sliced (use stems too)
2 (28 ounce) cans Italian tomatoes (Progresso brand is good)
1 (12 ounce) can tomato paste
1 tablespoon chili powder
1 tablespoon sugar
¼ teaspoon each of marjoram, oregano, basil, thyme
3 bay leaves
Salt and pepper to taste

Cook onion and garlic in butter and oil until clear. Add meat and brown. Stir in sliced mushrooms. Combine tomatoes, tomato paste and all seasonings; add to meat mixture. Simmer, uncovered, until thick; at least 3 hours. When cool, put in refrigerator. Before reheating to serve, or freezing, skim off fat. Serve over very thin spaghetti. Serves 10 to 12.

Lucy Jones
Louisville, Kentucky

SAUTÉED CHICKEN LIVERS WITH BRANDY

Excellent for breakfast or dinner

1 pound chicken livers
½ cup flour
½ teaspoon salt
½ teaspoon paprika
½ teaspoon freshly ground pepper
Pinch thyme
¼ cup butter, melted
6 ounces chicken broth (I use one packet of Romanoff's MBT Broth)
¼ cup brandy

Dredge chicken livers in flour that has been seasoned with salt, paprika, pepper and thyme. Sauté in butter over medium heat for 10 minutes; turn livers once to evenly brown. Add chicken broth and simmer about 5 minutes longer. Warm brandy. Light and pour over chicken livers. After flaming, stir and serve. Serves 4.

Goodwin C. Tyler
St. Paul, Minnesota

HAM BALLS

Flavorful

1½ pounds smoked ham, ground
1 pound lean ground pork
2 cups Waverly cracker crumbs
2 eggs, beaten
1 cup milk
Juice of 1 lemon and rind (finely grated)

Preheat oven to 325 degrees. Combine all ingredients and mix well. Shape into 16 balls. Place in a greased shallow baking dish.

Basting Sauce:

1 cup brown sugar
½ cup vinegar
½ cup water
1 teaspoon dry mustard

In a saucepan heat sugar, vinegar, water and mustard until dissolved. Pour over ham balls. Bake, uncovered, 1½ hours. Turn once. Serves 8.

Peggy Young
Centerville, Iowa

PORK CHOPS, CRANBERRIES AND APPLESAUCE

Bon Appetit!

6 pork chops, cut 1½ inches thick
1½ teaspoons salt
½ teaspoon freshly ground pepper
⅛ teaspoon thyme
2 eggs, beaten
1 cup dry bread crumbs
3 tablespoons butter
2 teaspoons chopped onion
1 cup applesauce
1 cup canned whole cranberries
½ cup hot water
1 tablespoon Worcestershire sauce
2 tablespoons sugar

Preheat oven to 350 degrees. Trim fat from chops; rub with mixture of the salt, pepper and thyme. Dip chops in eggs, then in crumbs, coating well. Melt butter in heavy skillet; sauté onions 2 minutes. Add chops and brown on both sides. Mix together the applesauce, cranberries, hot water, Worcestershire sauce and sugar. Pour over chops. Cover and bake for 50 minutes, or until chops are tender; remove cover for last 15 minutes. Serves 6.

Gordon Leland
Meriden, New Hampshire

CURRANT GLAZED PEACHES

1 (1 pound, 13 ounce) can peach halves
Brown sugar
Fresh lemon juice
2 tablespoons currant jelly

Drain peaches thoroughly and arrange, cup side up, in a shallow baking dish. Place a teaspoon of brown sugar in center of each peach, and drizzle about ½ teaspoon lemon juice in each. Broil about 4 inches from heat until lightly browned. Meanwhile melt jelly; spoon over browned peach halves, and broil a minute or two longer, until glazed. Serve hot with meats or poultry. Serves 5 to 6.

LAMB CARDINAL

Epicurean!

Thin slices cold cooked lamb
¼ cup currant jelly
¼ cup tarragon vinegar
½ cup tomato catsup
1 tablespoon butter
1 teaspoon Worcestershire
¼ teaspoon MSG
Salt and pepper to taste
1 tablespoon Marsala wine

In an iron skillet put the jelly, vinegar, catsup, butter, Worcestershire. Cook until jelly is melted and all is blended together. Add MSG, salt and pepper to taste. Add thin slices of lamb and cook, uncovered, over low heat for 20 minutes. Just before serving, add Marsala wine to the sauce. Stir. Serves 4 to 6.

LAMB AND WILD RICE CASSEROLE

Pamper your guests with this regal dish

2 pounds lamb cut in pieces
½ cup flour
1 teaspoon salt
½ teaspoon pepper
1 teaspoon paprika
½ stick butter
2 onions, grated
1 (1 pound) can tomatoes
1 pound fresh mushrooms, sliced
Lots of chopped parsley
1 cup sour cream
Rice (wild rice is excellent)

Preheat oven to 350 degrees. Mix together flour, salt, pepper and paprika. Put in paper bag; add lamb pieces and toss until lightly coated. In skillet, melt butter, add lamb and onions; brown. Transfer to a 2-quart casserole, add tomatoes and cook for 30 minutes. Add mushrooms and cook 30 minutes longer. Remove from oven. Put lots of chopped parsley on top, a large dollop of sour cream and serve over rice. Can be prepared ahead and reheated. Serves 6.

Carolyn McCluney
St. Louis, Missouri

TURKEY BREAST

Cooked in chicken broth and seasoned in a tangy marinade

1 (6 pound) frozen turkey breast
2 (10½ ounce) cans condensed chicken broth, undiluted
2 cups water
2 onions, each stuck with 4 whole cloves
1 celery stalk with leaves, cut up
4 medium size carrots, pared
2 teaspoons salt
10 whole peppercorns
1 bay leaf

Thaw and rinse turkey breast. In an 8-quart kettle, combine chicken broth, water, onions with cloves, celery, carrots, salt, peppercorns and bay leaf. Bring to boiling and add turkey breast. Bring back to boiling, reduce heat, and simmer, covered, for 2½ hours. Remove from heat. Let stand, frequently basting with broth, for 1½ hours, or until cool enough to handle; or refrigerate overnight, covered. Lift out turkey. Remove skin. Slice, cube, etc.

SAUTÉED DOVES

A real treat

12 whole doves
6 ounces butter
2 cups dry white wine
½ cup minced onion
4 tablespoons minced celery leaves
Salt and pepper to taste
1 teaspoon tarragon

In an electric skillet or large heavy iron pan, sauté doves in butter for 5 minutes or until lightly browned. Add wine, onion, celery leaves and salt and pepper. Cover and simmer over low heat for 45 minutes. Add tarragon and simmer for 15 minutes more, or until tender. Serves 4.

Fritz Gierhart
Vero Beach, Florida

ROAST WILD DUCK

Rare

Wild duck
Sweet milk
One small onion per duck
One small carrot per duck
¼ of an apple per duck
Two bacon strips per duck
Salt and freshly ground pepper to taste
Cumberland Sauce

Preheat oven to 500 degrees. Marinate duck in milk for 8 hours or overnight. With duck at room temperature, fill the cavity loosely with onion, carrot and apple. Lay bacon strips over duck breasts; add salt and pepper to taste. Place duck on rack in roasting pan and cook uncovered for 30 minutes. Discard cavity filling before serving. Carve and prepare dinner plates away from dining area. Serve with Cumberland Sauce. One wild duck serves 2.

Rollin Weary
Vero Beach, Florida

Cumberland Sauce:

1 tablespoon onion, finely chopped
1 cup red currant jelly
Zest of one orange and one lemon
3 tablespoons fresh lemon juice
3 tablespoons fresh orange juice
2 teaspoons Dijon mustard
1 cup port wine (such as Taylor or Tawny Port)
⅛ teaspoon powdered ginger
Dash cayenne pepper
Few grains salt

Boil onion in water for 3 minutes. Drain. In heavy saucepan melt jelly. Add onion, orange and lemon zest, lemon and orange juice and mustard. Simmer until smooth, about 10 minutes. Add wine, ginger, cayenne pepper and salt. Cook 5 minutes more, uncovered. Serve hot in a sauceboat. Sauce may be frozen or keeps under refrigeration for a long period of time.

Gloria Gossweiler
Rolle, Switzerland

INDIAN CURRY SAUCE

Served at the Indian Embassy in Washington

4 slices bacon, diced
¼ cup grated onion
¼ cup finely chopped celery
½ clove minced garlic
2 tablespoons vegetable oil
¼ cup flour, sifted
½ cup applesauce
3 teaspoons curry powder
3 tablespoons tomato paste
1 tablespoon sugar
1 tablespoon lemon juice
2 chicken bouillon cubes dissolved in 1¼ cups hot water
Salt to taste
1 cup light cream

In saucepan, sauté bacon until crisp. Remove bacon and bacon grease. Put onion, celery and garlic in vegetable oil and sauté for 10 minutes. Blend in flour and cook the mixture over low heat, stirring frequently, for 5 minutes. Add bacon and mix. Add applesauce, curry powder, tomato paste, sugar, lemon juice, bouillon cubes and water. Salt to taste. Cook the mixture, covered, over low heat for 45 minutes. To serve the curry sauce, add cream; stir. Add 3 cups cubed cooked chicken, turkey or cut-up shrimp. Heat the mixture through. Serve over steamed rice with the usual accompaniments. The sauce doubles easily and freezes well. Add cream and chicken just before serving. Suggested curry accompaniments: chutney, snipped parsley, sliced avocado, crisp bacon bits, chopped peanuts or toasted almonds, raisins, grated coconut, chopped cucumber. Serves 6.

Evelyn Searles
Harbor Springs, Michigan

PINEAPPLE PLEASURE

An excellent accompaniment to chicken, turkey, ham, pork

½ cup butter
4 slices white bread
½ cup sugar
3 tablespoons flour
3 eggs, beaten
1 (1 pound, 4 ounce) can unsweetened pineapple chunks, undrained

Preheat oven to 350 degrees. Melt butter in a saucepan over low heat. Cut crust from bread and cube. Add bread to melted butter; toss. Mix sugar and flour together, add eggs and blend well. Mix in pineapple with juice. Pour pineapple mixture into a 1½-quart buttered casserole. Sprinkle buttered bread cubes over top. Bake uncovered 50 to 60 minutes. Serve hot. Serves 4 to 6.

Anne Gregg
Vero Beach, Florida

PEACHES AND MINCEMEAT

Preheat oven to 300 degrees. Place canned peach halves in a buttered baking dish. Fill centers with mincemeat. Cover bottom of the dish with peach juice. Place in oven 15 to 20 minutes, or until hot.

PINEAPPLE CURRIED FRUIT

Really good! Serve with meats, fowl and wild game

1 (20 ounce) can pineapple chunks, unsweetened
1 teaspoon curry powder

Drain pineapple and reserve syrup. Place syrup in a heavy saucepan; stir in curry powder and mix well. Add pineapple. Cover and cook over medium heat until most of the juice is absorbed and mixture cooks down (about 1 hour). Stir occasionally; watch carefully the last few minutes of cooking and stir so it does not stick and burn bottom of pan. Serve hot or cold. Keeps well under refrigeration. Serves 3 to 4.

Peggy Fulenwider
Denver, Colorado

MUSHROOM BUSINESS

Delicious accompaniment for meat or fowl

1 pound fresh mushrooms, coarsely sliced
¼ cup butter
8 slices white bread, buttered
½ cup finely chopped onions
½ cup finely chopped celery
½ cup finely chopped green pepper
½ cup mayonnaise
¾ teaspoon salt
¾ teaspoon pepper
2 eggs, slightly beaten
1½ cups milk
1 (10¾ ounce) can mushroom soup, undiluted
½ cup shredded Cheddar cheese

Preheat oven to 300 degrees. Sauté mushrooms in butter. Cut 3 slices of bread into 1-inch squares and place in a 9x13-inch baking casserole. Combine the mushrooms with onions, celery, pepper, mayonnaise, salt and pepper and place on top of the bread squares. Cut 3 more slices of bread into 1-inch squares and place on top of the mushroom mixture. Combine eggs and milk and pour over all. Refrigerate several hours or overnight. An hour before cooking, spoon a can of mushroom soup over mixture; add 2 more slices of bread which have been cut into ½-inch squares and sprinkle cheese on top. Bake 60 to 70 minutes. Serves 8.

Helen Warren
Vero Beach, Florida

BARBEQUE SAUCE

A super sauce for chicken, ribs and beef

1 cup chili sauce
¼ cup cider vinegar
¼ cup Worcestershire
1 cup water
3 tablespoons lemon juice
4 tablespoons dark brown sugar
1 teaspoon chili powder
1 teaspoon celery seed
7 to 8 drops Tabasco
1 teaspoon salt
¼ teaspoon pepper

In a heavy saucepan combine all ingredients. Heat to boiling, stirring constantly. Simmer, uncovered, 10 to 15 minutes to blend flavors. Makes 2½ cups.

FETTUCCINE

Invite Alfredo . . . He'll love it

1 (8 ounce) package fettuccine green noodles
2 shallots, crushed with garlic press
1 tablespoon butter or margarine
1 cup chicken broth
½ cup heavy cream
1 cup sour cream
¼ cup freshly grated Parmesan cheese
1 tablespoon chives, chopped
Freshly ground pepper to taste
Fresh chopped parsley for garnish

Cook the fettuccine according to package directions. Drain thoroughly; rinse with cold water. Set aside. In a large saucepan, sauté the shallots in butter; stir in chicken broth and boil for 3 to 4 minutes. Remove from heat. Add heavy cream slowly. Add fettuccine, sour cream, Parmesan cheese, chives and ground pepper. Toss thoroughly. Return to low heat; stir until hot. Garnish with chopped parsley. Serve immediately. Serves 4.

GARLIC CHEESE GRITS

A true Southern dish . . .
a marvelous alternative to potatoes

1 cup grits
4 cups boiling water
1 teaspoon salt
½ cup butter
1 (6 ounce) roll garlic cheese
2 eggs, beaten
½ cup milk
Dash cayenne pepper
Corn flake crumbs
Butter to dot on crumbs

Preheat oven to 350 degrees. Cook grits in boiling, salted water until thick. Remove from heat. Stir in butter and cheese until melted. Mix egg, milk and pepper; add to grits and stir well. Pour into buttered casserole and cover with corn flake crumbs. Dot with butter. Bake, uncovered, 45 to 55 minutes. Serves 6.

BANANA SCALLOPS

Good served with a meat course

Vegetable oil
1 teaspoon salt
1 egg, slightly beaten *or* ¼ cup evaporated milk
6 firm bananas
¾ cup crushed corn flakes

For deep fat frying have deep kettle ½ to ⅔ full of vegetable oil. For shallow frying have 1-inch of vegetable oil in frying pan. Heat oil to 375, or until a 1 inch cube of bread will brown in about 40 seconds. It is important to have oil at correct temperature before frying. Add salt to egg or undiluted evaporated milk. Peel bananas and slice crosswise into pieces 1 inch thick. Dip into egg or milk. Drain. Roll in corn flake crumbs. Fry in hot oil 1½ to 2 minutes, or until brown and tender. Drain well. Serve very hot. Serves 6.

MY FAVORITE BAKED BEANS

4 cups Great Northern beans
1 cup sugar
1 tablespoon salt
1 pound salt pork, cut-up in 1-inch pieces

Soak beans overnight. When ready to cook, preheat oven to 250 degrees. Drain beans. Place beans in a large roaster; mix in sugar, salt and salt pork. Barely cover with water. Bake, covered, all day, about 8 hours. As needed, add boiling water, a cup at a time. Uncover the last hour. Serves 8 to 10.

Mary June Burd
Bethesda, Maryland

STUFFED SWEET POTATOES BOURBON

Tasty with cold sliced ham, beef or pork

4 medium size yams (if sweet potatoes are available, omit white potato)
1 large white Idaho baking potato
½ cup butter, softened
2 ounces bourbon
Salt, freshly ground pepper, to taste
Heavy cream as needed
½ cup ground pecans for topping

Preheat oven to 425 degrees. Bake the 5 potatoes for 1 hour or until soft. Turn off oven. Slice off the top third of the yams. Remove the filling of the 5 potatoes and force through a potato ricer onto the softened butter in a bowl. Add the bourbon, salt and pepper and beat with a fork or whisk until fluffy. Add a small amount of heavy cream if needed. Refill the 4 yam skins with the mixture. Top with ground pecans and refrigerate. Reheat at 350 (preheat) for about 40 minutes. Serves 4.

Sheila Manning
Vero Beach, Florida

TWICE BAKED POTATOES

Do keep your freezer filled with these—really good!

8 large baking potatoes
Vegetable oil
¼ cup butter or margarine
1 cup sour cream
1 egg, beaten
1½ teaspoons salt
⅛ teaspoon white pepper
Paprika

Preheat oven to 400 degrees. Rub potatoes with vegetable oil. Bake on a rack for 1 hour. Cut a long oval slice from potatoes; scoop out pulp. Combine butter, sour cream, egg, salt and pepper; blend well. Add to potato pulp and mix thoroughly. Pile filling back into 6 shells, piling high. Sprinkle with paprika. Wrap in foil and place in plastic bags; freeze. To serve, it is unnecessary to thaw. Preheat oven to 400 degrees. Remove foil, place potato on rack; heat thoroughly, about 40 minutes. Serves 6.

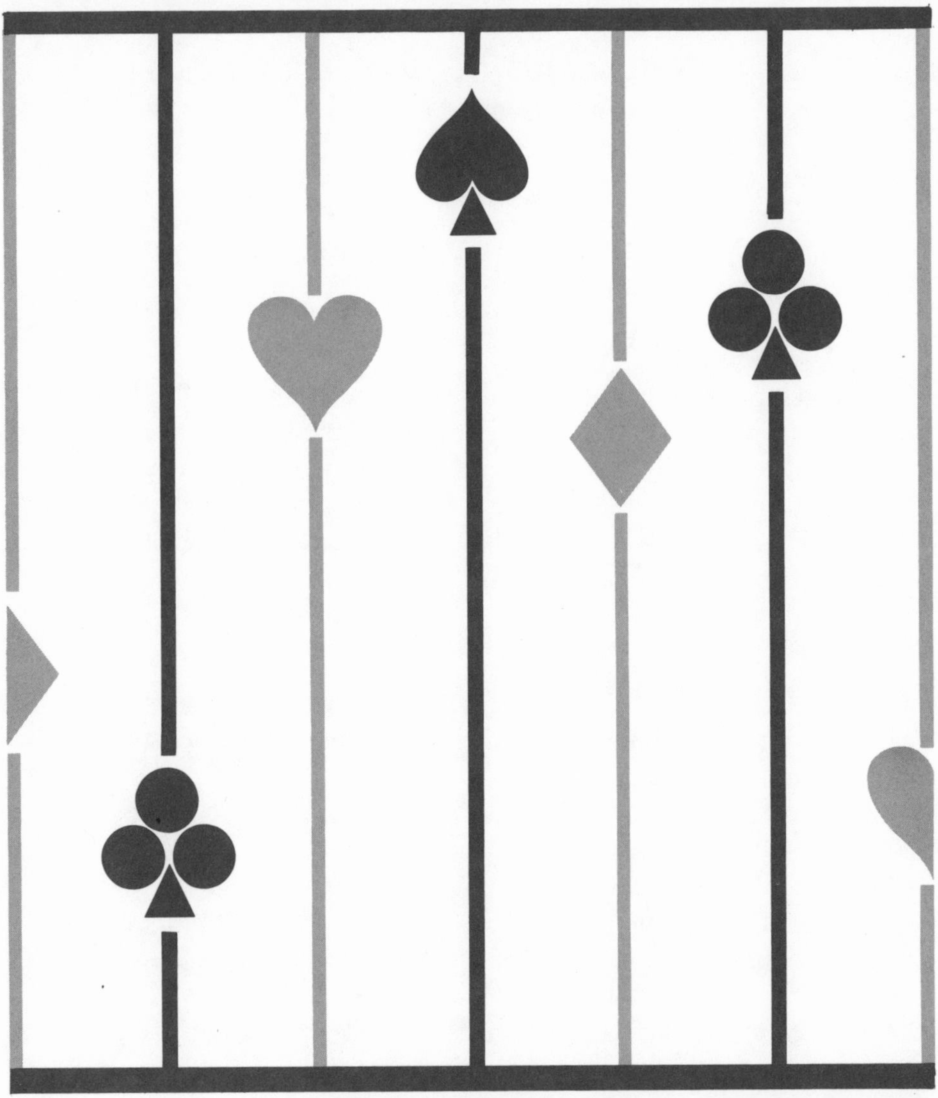

VEGETABLES

ARTICHOKE BOTTOMS AU GRATIN

Perfect dish for special occasions

1 (15 ounce) can artichoke bottoms
1 teaspoon Worcestershire sauce
Pinch of nutmeg
Dash cayenne pepper
Cheddar cheese sauce
Parmesan cheese, grated

Preheat oven to 300 degrees. Grease shallow casserole. Drain and rinse artichoke bottoms; put in prepared casserole. Combine Worcestershire sauce, nutmeg, cayenne pepper with Cheddar cheese sauce and pour over artichoke bottoms. Sprinkle with grated Parmesan cheese and bake for 30 minutes or until casserole is bubbly. Brown under broiler and serve at once.

Cheddar Cheese Sauce:

3 tablespoons butter
3 tablespoons flour
1½ cups hot milk
¾ cup shredded Cheddar cheese
Salt and pepper to taste

Melt butter over medium heat. Add flour and stir for 3 to 4 minutes. Pour in hot milk and continue to stir rapidly until sauce is smooth. Continue to stir until sauce comes to a boil. Lower heat and gently simmer and stir 3 to 4 minutes longer. Add cheese and stir only until it is melted. Season to taste. Serves 4.

Sheila Huidekoper
Nonquitt, Massachusetts

BESSIE PICKENS' STEWED TOMATOES

Everyone has a second helping!

3 (14½ ounce) cans stewed tomatoes, top quality
2 heaping tablespoons dark brown sugar
2 chopped green onions, using tops
2 slices white bread with crust
Salt and pepper to taste

Preheat oven to 350 degrees. Pour tomatoes into a shallow buttered baking dish (8½ x 8½ inches). Sprinkle brown sugar and onions over top. Tear bread slices into small pieces and add to tomato mixture. Mix together. Bake at least 1 hour, or until bubbling and liquid has been absorbed. Serves 4 to 5.

Peggy Fulenwider
Denver, Colorado

BROCCOLI CHEESE CASSEROLE

If you like broccoli AND bleu cheese AND cream cheese, you'll love this!

2 tablespoons butter
2 tablespoons flour
¼ teaspoon salt
1 (3 ounce) package cream cheese, softened
¼ cup bleu cheese, crumbled
1 cup milk
2 (10 ounce) packages frozen chopped broccoli, cooked and drained
10 to 12 round buttery crackers, crushed

Preheat oven to 350 degrees. In a large saucepan, melt butter; add flour, salt, cream cheese and bleu cheese. Blend well. Add milk; cook and stir until mixture bubbles. Stir in cooked broccoli. Turn into a 1-quart casserole. Top with crushed crumbs. Bake 30 minutes. Serves 6 to 8.

Margaret Cooper
Winnetka, Illinois

BLOSSOM'S DELECTABLE SPINACH CASSEROLE

4 (10 ounce) packages frozen chopped spinach
½ cup butter, melted
2 (8 ounce) packages cream cheese, softened
1 (8½ ounce) can artichoke hearts, drained and quartered
1 (6 ounce) can water chestnuts, drained and thinly sliced
2 teaspoons onion powder (or more)
Cayenne pepper and black pepper to taste
Pepperidge Farm herb dressing mix
⅓ cup freshly grated Parmesan cheese

Preheat oven to 350 degrees. Thaw spinach and drain well. Add butter, cream cheese, artichoke hearts, water chestnuts and onion powder, tasting frequently. Add cayenne and black pepper to mixture; blend thoroughly. Place in a 2-quart casserole, cover with herb dressing and sprinkle with Parmesan cheese. Bake 30 to 40 minutes or until very hot. Serves 12.

Peggy Carr
Les Cheneaux Club
Cedarville, Michigan

CORN PUDDING

A delicious accompaniment

6 ears corn
½ cup butter, melted
5 eggs
2 cups half and half cream
1 tablespoon sugar
Salt and pepper to taste

Preheat oven to 300 degrees. Grate corn very thin (no hulls in mixture). Add corn to melted butter. Beat eggs and fold into corn; then add cream, sugar, salt and pepper. Bake in a casserole set in a pan of water for 1 hour and 15 minutes. Serves 8.

Margaret Hanes
Atlanta, Georgia

CAULIFLOWER WITH SHRIMP AND PECANS

Elegant and delicious

1 medium size cauliflower
⅓ cup broken pecans
2 tablespoons butter, melted
1 (10 ounce) can frozen cream of shrimp soup, thawed
4 ounces sour cream
Red food coloring (optional)

Trim cauliflower; wash thoroughly. Place whole head in a small amount of salted boiling water. Cover and cook about 20 minutes, until just tender. Drain. Over low heat, cook pecans in butter until lightly brown. Set aside. Heat thawed soup in saucepan; fold in sour cream. If red food coloring is used, add a drop. Put hot cauliflower in serving dish, pour shrimp soup over top and sprinkle with pecans. Serves 6.

Dottie Neville
Jupiter, Florida

FILLED ZUCCHINI

Very tasty

6 zucchini (6 inches long)
3 tablespoons butter
¼ pound mushrooms, diced
1 carrot, grated
2 tablespoons minced onion
½ teaspoon salt
¼ teaspoon pepper
½ cup shredded Cheddar cheese
¼ cup water

Preheat oven to 375 degrees. Cut zucchini in half; scoop out pulp and dice. Sauté in butter with mushrooms, carrot, onion, salt and pepper. Stir in cheese. Fill shells, place in narrow baking dish and pour water around zucchini. Cover with foil. Bake for 30 minutes. Serves 6.

Margaret Cooper
Winnetka, Illinois

CELERY CASSEROLE

Unusual and crunchy

4 cups celery, diced
¼ cup almonds, slivered and blanched
½ cup water chestnuts, sliced
1 (4 ounce) can mushrooms, sliced
5 tablespoons butter
3 tablespoons flour
1 cup chicken broth
¾ cup half and half cream
½ cup grated Parmesan cheese
½ cup soft bread crumbs
3 tablespoons melted butter

Preheat oven to 350 degrees. Cook celery in boiling water, uncovered, for 5 minutes. Drain. Mix with almonds, chestnuts and mushrooms. Melt butter in a saucepan; add flour and cook roux until it bubbles; add chicken broth and cream. Cook over medium heat until thick. Blend celery mixture into the sauce. Pour into a greased, ovenproof 12x8x2-inch casserole. Combine bread crumbs and cheese. Sprinkle on top. Drizzle melted butter over mixture. Bake for 25 minutes, uncovered, or until hot and bubbly. Serves 8.

Peggy Young
Centerville, Iowa

TORTA DI MELANZANA

(Eggplant Pie)
Serve with roast beef and a green salad

First layer:

1 medium size eggplant, thinly sliced
Vegetable oil
½ teaspoon salt
½ teaspoon white pepper
3 tablespoons parsley, finely minced
Good pinch thyme

Spread eggplant on paper towels, sprinkle well with salt; let steep for 30 minutes. Dry. Sauté eggplant in hot oil until soft and delicately browned. Season with pepper. Place layers of eggplant slices in a 9 or 10-inch pyrex pie dish. Sprinkle parsley and thyme over top.

Second layer:

1 (28 ounce) can Italian-style pear-shaped tomatoes, sliced and drained well
½ teaspoon salt
½ teaspoon white pepper
3 tablespoons finely minced parsley
4 tablespoons finely chopped onions
3 tablespoons finely chopped green pepper

Place tomatoes on top of eggplant layer. Sprinkle with salt and pepper. Sprinkle parsley, onions and pepper over all.

Third layer:

½ pound Mozzarella cheese

Cover the tomatoes with slices of cheese.

Fourth layer:

3 egg yolks
¼ cup milk
Parmesan cheese, freshly grated

Add egg yolks to milk and beat very well. Pour mixture over pie. Bake in a preheated 325 degree oven 25 to 30 minutes, or until custard is firm and the cheese slightly browned. Cut the torta in wedges and serve with a bowl of freshly grated Parmesan cheese on the side. Serves 6 to 8.

Alyce Grove
Chester, Nova Scotia

SQUASH MEDLEY

A much praised vegetable casserole

2 pounds yellow squash or zucchini, thinly sliced
½ cup butter
½ package prepared herb stuffing mix
1 (10¾ ounce) can cream of chicken soup
1 onion, chopped fine
1 (8 ounce) carton sour cream
1 (6 ounce) can water chestnuts, sliced thin
Salt and pepper to taste

Preheat oven to 350 degrees. Steam squash until barely tender (it should not be soft). Mix butter with stuffing. Put ½ of the butter-stuffing mixture in a 2-quart buttered casserole. Mix all other ingredients together and add to casserole. Sprinkle other ½ of butter-stuffing mixture on top. Bake 30 minutes. Serves 8.

Marguerite Neel Williams
Thomasville, Georgia

"WEINKRAUT"

Welcome this old friend in a new guise

1 small onion, grated
¼ cup butter, melted
2 tablespoons brown sugar
½ teaspoon salt
1 teaspoon vinegar
1½ cups dry white wine
1 cup chicken broth
1 small potato, grated
1 quart sauerkraut, drained

In a large saucepan, add grated onion to butter and cook until just tender. Add sugar; stir until melted. Add all other ingredients and cook, uncovered, for 30 minutes. Serves 6.

Elaine Putney
Vero Beach, Florida

TOMATO SOUFFLÉ

Delicate flavor

2 tablespoons butter
1 clove garlic, pressed
2 tablespoons flour
2 cups milk, scalded
1 teaspoon salt
1 teaspoon Worcestershire sauce
1 bay leaf
6 tablespoons tomato paste
Pinch of sugar
6 eggs, separated

Preheat oven to 350 degrees. Melt butter in a saucepan; add garlic and cook about 1 minute. Over low heat, blend in flour, stirring 2 to 3 minutes until well blended and the taste of raw flour has vanished; add milk gradually, stirring with wire whisk until the sauce is thickened and smooth. Add salt, Worcestershire, bay leaf, tomato paste and sugar. Cook 5 to 6 minutes. Remove from heat; discard bay leaf. Beat egg yolks; add a small amount of hot sauce and blend well. Combine egg yolks with the remaining hot sauce. Beat the egg whites until stiff; gently fold them into the sauce. Pour soufflé mixture into a 3-quart soufflé dish and set the dish in a pan of water. Bake 50 to 60 minutes until soufflé is puffed and browned. Test by inserting a silver knife part way into center of soufflé; if it comes out clean, soufflé is done. Serve immediately. Serves 6.

Jane Robertson
Ocean Ridge, Florida

AMANDINE GARNISH

Excellent with fish, green beans, etc.

½ cup butter
½ cup almonds, slivered
1 teaspoon lemon juice

Melt butter; add almonds. Stir and sauté over low heat until lightly browned. Remove from heat and stir in lemon juice.

EL DIABLO MUSTARD

1 loosely packed cup of good dry mustard
1 cup cider vinegar
1 cup sugar
3 whole eggs, beaten

Soak mustard and vinegar for 12 hours. Add sugar and eggs and cook in the top of a double boiler over simmering water for 20 minutes. Beat frequently with hand beater to prevent lumping. Place in sterile jars, cover and refrigerate. It will keep indefinitely under refrigeration. Delicious with ham, hot dogs, etc. Good as an appetizer with small chunks of sharp Cheddar speared with a toothpick. Makes about 1 pint.

Lazelle Rafferty
Little Compton, Rhode Island

COCKTAIL SAUCE

½ cup chili sauce
½ cup catsup
2 tablespoons chopped green pepper
2 tablespoons chopped onion
½ teaspoon dry mustard
½ teaspoon salt
1½ tablespoons horseradish
1 teaspoon ground black pepper
2 teaspoons Worcestershire sauce

Combine all ingredients and mix thoroughly. Chill before using. Makes about 1¼ cups.

JEZEBEL SAUCE

Delicious with any meat, hot or cold and good with cream cheese and crackers too

1 (10 ounce) jar apple jelly
1 (10 ounce) jar pineapple preserves
1 (5 ounce) jar moist horseradish
½ teaspoon dry mustard
Few grindings black pepper

Mix all ingredients thoroughly. Refrigerate. The sauce will keep for months under refrigeration.

Alice McCue
Vero Beach, Florida

BLENDER HOLLANDAISE SAUCE

Really delicious

4 egg yolks
2 tablespoons lemon juice
A pinch of cayenne pepper
¼ teaspoon salt
1 cup butter

Have ready in your blender egg yolks, juice, pepper and salt. Heat butter to bubbly stage but do not brown. Cover blender and turn motor on "high". After 3 seconds, remove the lid and pour the melted butter over the eggs in a steady stream. By the time the butter has been poured in (about 30 seconds), the sauce should be finished. If not, blend on "high" about 5 seconds longer. Serve at once. This sauce may be frozen and reconstituted over hot water. Makes about 1½ cups.

BREADS

"PANAMA LIMITED" FRENCH TOAST

Superb!

2 eggs, beaten
½ cup milk
2 slices bread, cut 1½ inches thick, crust removed, and cut diagonally to form triangular shaped pieces
3 cups shortening
Confectioners' sugar

Mix together the eggs and milk and beat well. Dip the bread slices in egg and milk mixture. Fry in hot shortening in a deep fat fryer or a medium size frying pan. Drain the cooked toast. Sprinkle liberally with confectioners' sugar. Serve hot.

Illinois Central Railroad

PERPETUAL MUFFINS

Take 6 to 8 to a friend—a lovely treat

2 cups All-Bran cereal
1 cup Bran Buds cereal
1 cup boiling water
2 cups buttermilk
1½ cups sugar
2 eggs, beaten
½ cup vegetable oil
2½ cups flour
2½ teaspoons soda
½ teaspoon salt

In a large bowl, mix cereals together. Pour water over cereals. Add buttermilk, sugar, eggs and oil. Mix. Sift together flour, soda and salt. Add to cereal mixture. Stir until just mixed; do not overmix. Cover bowl and refrigerate. Muffin batter keeps 6 weeks. Do not stir again. When ready to cook, place batter in a greased muffin tin in a cold oven. Set oven to 400 degrees and bake 20 minutes. A few raisins may be added to the batter or for a special treat add frozen or fresh blueberries. Makes enough batter for 36 muffins.

Fleur Piper
San Antonio, Texas

SOUR CREAM CRESCENTS

Home made rolls! These are wonderful!

1 cup sour cream
1½ packages active dry yeast
⅓ cup warm water
1 cup butter or margarine, softened
½ cup sugar
½ teaspoon salt
4 cups flour, sifted
2 eggs, well beaten

Heat sour cream in the top of a double boiler over simmering water until it becomes slightly yellow around edges. (Separation of cream will not affect product.) Meanwhile, soften yeast in warm water; let stand 5 to 10 minutes. Put butter, sugar and salt into a large bowl. Immediately pour heated sour cream over ingredients in bowl and stir mixture until butter is completely melted. When mixture has cooled to lukewarm, blend in 1 cup of the flour, beating until smooth. Stir softened yeast and add, mixing well. Add 1 cup of the remaining flour and beat until smooth. Add eggs and beat until thoroughly blended. Add remaining 2 cups flour; again, beat thoroughly. Cover bowl and put into refrigerator 6 hours or overnight. (There is no time limit at this point, and any remaining dough can be wrapped in foil and used as needed.) Divide dough into fourths. On a lightly floured surface, roll each portion into a round ¼ inch thick. Cut each round into 12 wedge-shaped pieces. Roll up each wedge beginning at wide end. Place rolls on greased baking sheets with points underneath. Curve into crescents. Let stand in a warm place until light, 1 hour or a little more. Do not cover. Instead of crescents, Parker House rolls will do. Bake 15 minutes in a preheated 375 degree oven, or until golden brown. Makes 4 dozen.

Lilli Jackson
Opelika, Alabama

NEVER-FAIL POPOVERS

Eat some . . . freeze some

1 cup milk
1 cup flour, sifted
1 tablespoon melted butter
½ teaspoon salt
2 eggs, well beaten

Set oven to 425 degrees—DO NOT PREHEAT. Butter and lightly flour 6 glass custard cups (I use Baker's Joy . . . excellent). Have all ingredients at room temperature. Combine milk, flour, butter and salt. Beat with an electric beater until smooth. By hand, stir in beaten eggs, blending well. (Do not overbeat.) Fill cups ⅔ full. Bake at once. Set cups on a cookie sheet in a cold oven. Bake 45 minutes. Remove from oven; insert a sharp paring knife gently into the popovers to allow steam to escape. Return to oven for 2 minutes to dry out. To freeze; wrap cooled popovers in aluminum foil or place in plastic bags. To reheat; unwrap and place in preheated 375 degree oven. Heat 5 to 7 minutes. They will taste as good as just-made. Makes 6.

Dottie Watts
Kenilworth, Illinois

POPOVER PANCAKE

It's fun to watch it pop and it's mighty good too!

½ cup all-purpose flour
½ cup milk
2 eggs, slightly beaten
¼ cup butter
2 tablespoons confectioners' sugar
Juice of ½ lemon

Preheat oven to 425 degrees. In mixing bowl combine flour, milk and eggs. Beat lightly. The batter will be slightly lumpy. Put butter into a 12-inch round frying pan with heatproof handle. Place in oven until very hot. Pour in the batter, return to oven, and bake 20 minutes or until pancake is puffed all around sides of the pan and golden brown. Remove from oven and sprinkle with confectioners' sugar and lemon juice. Serve immediately. Serves 2 to 3.

CAPE COD CRANBERRY NUT LOAF

My Christmas present one year—one of my favorite gifts

2 cups all-purpose flour
1½ teaspoons baking powder
½ teaspoon soda
1 teaspoon salt
2 tablespoons butter, melted
⅞ cup orange juice
1 egg, beaten
⅞ cup white sugar
3 tablespoons light brown sugar
1 tablespoon grated orange rind (optional)
1 cup whole cranberries, uncooked
Flour
½ cup chopped walnuts

Preheat oven to 350 degrees. Sift together flour, baking powder, soda and salt. Set aside. Melt butter and add to orange juice. In a large bowl, stir together egg, white sugar and light brown sugar. Add flour mixture and orange juice mix alternately to egg and sugar, starting and ending with flour. Add grated orange rind. Fold in cranberries which have been lightly floured; add walnuts. Bake 1 hour in a greased and floured 9x5-inch loaf pan. Invert. Keep in refrigerator or freeze.

Grace O'Keeffe
Osterville, Massachusetts

KAVLI FLATBROD

Norwegian Flatbread—Delicious with soups and salads

9 pieces of Norwegian flatbread, thin
1½ tablespoons butter, softened
½ teaspoon Beau Monde seasoning
4 drops Worcestershire sauce

Preheat oven to 325 degrees. Combine butter, Beau Monde and Worcestershire sauce; spread on flatbread. Place on a cookie sheet; bake 5 minutes. Cool before serving.

Arnfinn Jackson Sveen
Franklin, North Carolina

DILLY BREAD

1½ packets dry yeast
½ cup warm water
2 cups cream cottage cheese, large curd
4 tablespoons sugar or honey
2 tablespoons dry onion flakes
2 tablespoons butter
3 teaspoons dill *weed*
1½ teaspoons salt
½ teaspoon soda
2 eggs, beaten
4½ to 5 cups flour (I use a mixture of white and wheat)
Melted butter

Soften yeast in water. Heat cottage cheese to just lukewarm. Add sugar, onion, butter, dill weed, salt, soda, eggs and softened yeast. Add 2 cups flour and beat well. Add more flour; turn out on board and knead for 10 minutes. (This dough will be slightly sticky). Put into greased bowl and let rise until double. Punch down and let rise again. Punch down; divide into loaves. Put into very well greased 9x5x3-inch pans. Let rise until double. Bake in a preheated 350 degree oven about 50 minutes. Cover with foil after first 20 minutes. Turn out of pans on rack to cool. Brush with melted butter. Makes 2 loaves.

Martha Orr Hassel
Wilmette, Illinois

CORN BISCUITS

So easy and so good

½ cup butter or margarine
1½ cups Bisquick
1 (8 ounce) can cream corn

Preheat oven to 400 degrees. Melt butter or margarine in a 13x9-inch baking pan. Combine Bisquick and corn. Drop batter by teaspoonful into baking pan; turn over to coat all sides. Bake 15 to 20 minutes. Watch after 15 minutes; they should be lightly browned. Serve hot. Makes 2 dozen.

Blanche Evans
Vero Beach, Florida

FRENCH BREAD WITH HERB BUTTER

Be organized
Double the recipe . . . eat one . . . freeze one

½ cup butter
1 tablespoon dry parsley
1 tablespoon dry chives
2 teaspoons dry sweet basil
½ teaspoon lemon juice
3 dashes Tabasco
Medium size loaf of French bread

Preheat oven to 350 degrees. Soften butter. Add herbs and seasonings and mix well. Cut the bread in thin slices but do not slice it all the way through; leave the bottom crust undisturbed. Butter each slice generously. Wrap the bread in aluminum foil and warm in oven for a few minutes. Just before serving, open the foil for a short time to brown crust. Makes 1 loaf.

ZUCCHINI BREAD

Very good

3 eggs, beaten
1 cup salad oil
1 cup sugar
1 cup firmly packed brown sugar
3 teaspoons maple flavoring
2 cups coarsely shredded zucchini (3 medium size)
2½ cups flour
2 teaspoons soda
½ teaspoon baking powder
2 teaspoons salt
3 teaspoons cinnamon
½ cup wheat germ
⅓ cup sesame seeds
1 cup pecan or walnut nutmeats, coarsely chopped

Preheat oven to 350 degrees. To eggs add oil, sugars and maple flavoring. Beat until foamy and thick. Add zucchini stirring in with a spoon. Mix together the flour, soda, baking powder, salt, cinnamon, wheat germ, sesame seeds and nutmeats. Add flour mixture to the batter and stir until just blended. Pour into 2 greased and floured 8½x4½-inch loaf pans. Bake for 1 hour or until tester comes out clean. Cool in pan for 10 minutes. The bread improves with a few days "aging" in refrigerator. Slices well when cold. Freezes well.

Barbara Morrison
Vero Beach, Florida

RAISIN BEER BREAD

You'll never buy another loaf—toast for breakfast

3 cups self-rising flour, sifted
2 tablespoons sugar
1 cup dark seedless raisins
1 can beer, room temperature
1 tablespoon butter, melted

Preheat oven to 375 degrees. Mix together flour, sugar and raisins. Add beer and stir thoroughly to make a dough. Bake in a greased 8x4½-inch loaf pan for 55 minutes. Turn out and brush with melted butter. Freezes well.

Evelyn Converse
Vero Beach, Florida

GRAHAM BREAD

Toasted . . . a nice way to start a day!

¾ cup dark seedless raisins
1 cup water plus 2 tablespoons water
1½ cups graham flour (wheat)
1½ cups Quaker Oats, regular
1½ cups bran flakes
1½ cups sugar
1 teaspoon salt
1½ teaspoons soda
1½ cups buttermilk
2 eggs, well beaten
1 tablespoon salad oil

Preheat oven to 300 degrees. Simmer raisins and water together for 10 minutes. Cool. Mix dry ingredients in a large bowl. Blend buttermilk, eggs and oil; add to dry ingredients. Add raisins plus water. Mix thoroughly. Turn into a greased, 9x5-inch loaf pan. Fill ⅔ full. Bake 75 to 90 minutes. Keeps very well.

BANANA BREAD

This has been one of my favorites for years!

1 cup sugar
½ cup butter
2 eggs, beaten
3 tablespoons buttermilk
1 cup mashed bananas (about 3)
2 cups flour, sifted
1 teaspoon baking soda
½ teaspoon salt
½ cup pecans, chopped

Preheat oven to 350 degrees. Cream sugar and butter. Add eggs, buttermilk and bananas. Add flour, baking soda and salt, stirring just enough to mix. Fold in pecans. Pour into 2 greased 7½x3½-inch loaf pans. Bake 45 minutes. Cool 15 to 20 minutes. Remove from pans to cooling rack. Freezes well. Makes 2 loaves.

Cherry Sue Jackson
Opelika, Alabama

PUMPKIN NUT BREAD

Excellent

3 cups sugar
3½ cups flour, unsifted
1 teaspoon baking powder
2 teaspoons soda
1½ teaspoons salt
¾ teaspoon cinnamon
¾ teaspoon nutmeg
¾ teaspoon allspice
½ teaspoon cloves
4 eggs, well beaten
1 cup vegetable oil
⅔ cup water
1 (1 pound) can pumpkin
1 cup coarsely chopped walnuts or pecans

Preheat oven to 350 degrees. Mix all the dry ingredients in a large bowl. Add eggs, oil, water and pumpkin; mix until well blended. Add nuts. Pour the batter into 4 buttered and floured 7½x3½-inch loaf pans. Bake 50 to 60 minutes, or until a toothpick inserted in the center comes out clean. Cool for 10 minutes; remove to a rack, Freezes well. Makes 4 loaves.

Helen Warren
Vero Beach, Florida

ALMOND COFFEE CAKE

Make this for a special treat

1 (8 ounce) can almond paste
¼ cup sugar
1 cup butter, softened
2 eggs, beaten
1 cup sour cream or King Sour
1 teaspoon vanilla
2 cups flour, sifted
1 teaspoon baking powder
¾ teaspoon salt

Preheat oven to 325 degrees. In a large mixing bowl cut up almond paste and add sugar. Cream with fingers until smooth, no lumps remaining. Using an electric beater gradually add butter; add eggs, sour cream and vanilla. On low speed, fold the flour, baking powder and salt into the sour cream mixture. Blend well.

Topping:

½ cup blanched almonds, slivered
¼ cup firmly packed dark brown sugar
¼ cup butter
¼ cup flour

Mix the almonds with brown sugar, butter and flour until crumbly. Sprinkle this mixture into a 6-cup Bundt tube pan which has been sprayed with aerosol vegetable oil spray or buttered and floured. Pour in the batter. Fill the pan right to the top; it will not spill over. A 10-inch angel food tube pan may be used; the cake will not be as high. If the angel food pan is used, pour the batter into the buttered and floured pan and sprinkle the almond topping over all. Bake 1 hour or until a toothpick inserted in the center comes out clean. Let stand after baking 15 to 20 minutes; invert on rack to complete cooling. Serves 10 to 12. Freezes well.

ANGEL BISCUITS

Delicious—serve hot with sweet butter and jelly

1 package yeast
2 tablespoons warm water
1 teaspoon sugar
5 cups flour
1 extra cup flour, set aside
3 teaspoons baking powder
1 teaspoon soda
¼ cup sugar
1 teaspoon salt
1 cup soft shortening
2 cups buttermilk

Preheat oven to 400 degrees. Dissolve yeast in warm water and 1 teaspoon sugar; set aside. In a large mixing bowl sift together 5 cups flour, baking powder, soda, sugar and salt. Cut in the shortening until well blended. Add yeast and buttermilk and mix with a spoon, then by hand, until smooth. Add more flour, as needed. Place dough in a large greased bowl, turning over to grease all sides. Roll the dough with a lightly floured rolling pin or pat it gently with the palm of the hand until it has the desired thickness; about ⅓ inch for a plain biscuit and 1 inch or more for shortcake. Cut with biscuit cutter and place on lightly greased baking sheet. Bake 12 to 15 minutes. The dough will keep for a week under refrigeration. Makes about 7 dozen.

Elaine Putney
Vero Beach, Florida

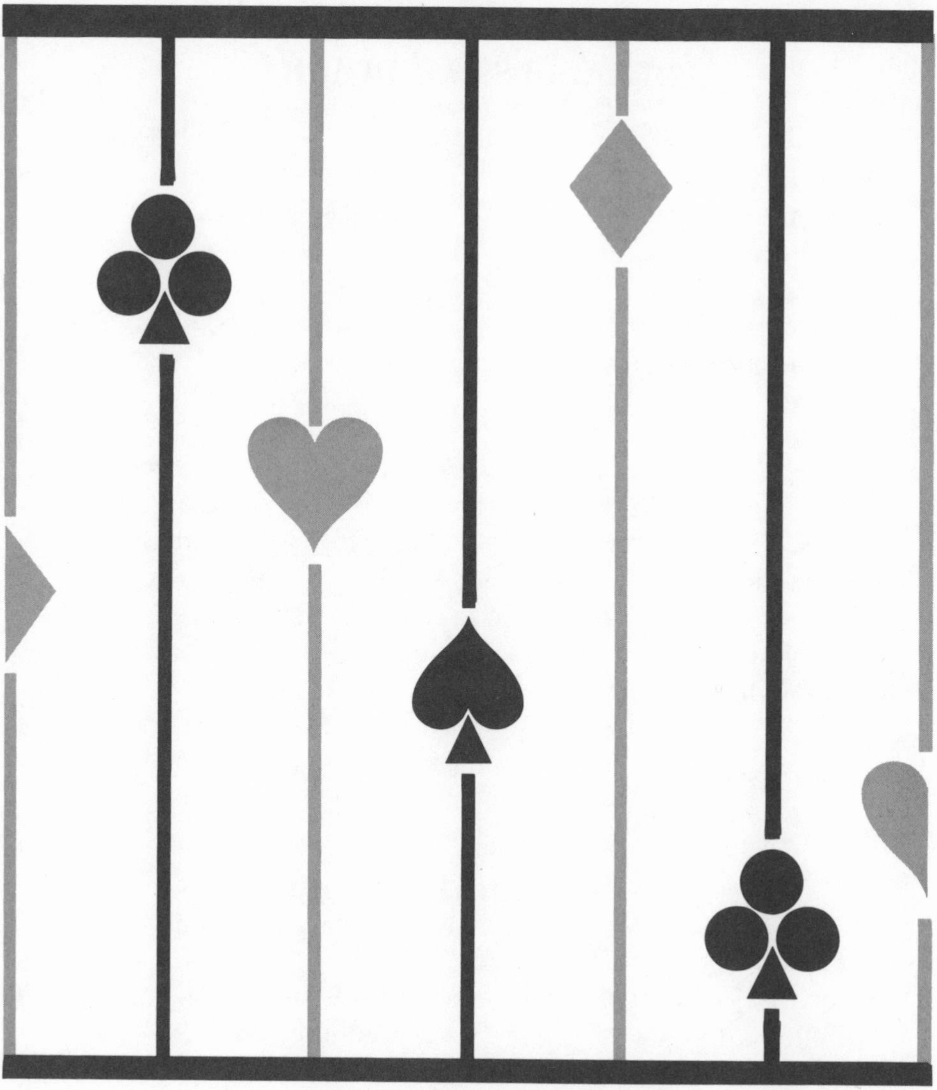

SANDWICHES

BREADLESS SANDWICH

The Earl would have liked this!

1 head lettuce
1 cup mayonnaise
¼ cup creamy Italian dressing
Slices of tomatoes
Slices of cooked chicken breasts
1 cup shredded sharp Cheddar cheese
Fresh Parmesan cheese, grated

For each of 4 sandwiches, place a ¾ inch slice of lettuce on a baking pan. Mix mayonnaise and Italian dressing and put 2 tablespoons over each lettuce slice. Top with tomato and chicken slices. Mix Cheddar cheese with remaining dressing and cover each sandwich with this mixture; sprinkle each with grated Parmesan cheese Place 3 inches under broiler until cheese melts. Serves 4.

Lucy Jones
Vero Beach, Florida

BROILED MUSHROOM SANDWICHES

Delicious for a bridge luncheon or a company snack

1 cup finely chopped fresh mushrooms
2 tablespoons butter
12 thin slices bread, lightly buttered
12 slices tomatoes, ½ inch thick
¼ pound sharp cheese, shredded
1 egg, slightly beaten
½ teaspoon salt
6 strips bacon

Sauté mushrooms in butter for 5 minutes. Use a large cookie cutter and cut circles from bread. Top with tomato slice. Mix cheese, egg, salt and mushrooms together and spread over tomato. Cut bacon strip in half and place a piece on each sandwich. Place under broiler until cheese mixture is bubbly and bacon crisp. Serves 6.

CLUB SANDWICHES FOR TWELVE

Without having a nervous breakdown

This is a great bridge luncheon or fine for a Sunday night supper. It can be prepared ahead of time, only adding bacon and toast at the last minute. Arrange the platters, cover with plastic wrap and place in the refrigerator for 3 or 4 hours.

6 frying chicken breasts, cooked. (I simmer mine in Campbell's chicken broth, but they may be baked). Slice.
36 slices of bacon (if baked in a 350 oven, they won't need watching).
4 to 6 heads Bibb lettuce
Dish of pickles, black and green olives, radishes, and anything else that comes to mind.
12 to 14 tomatoes, peeled and sliced, but not too thin.
24 slices of white bread, toasted and buttered, served in a basket.
Separate bowl of mayonnaise (homemade if possible, but Hellmann's is good).

Use two large platters. On one place chicken and bacon. On the other put lettuce and tomatoes. Have the basket of hot toast on buffet and the pickles, olives and radishes in a dish alongside bowl of mayonnaise. Everyone does his/her own thing from here.

Helen Hecht
Scottsdale, Arizona

POLLY'S PARTY SANDWICHES

Swiss Tuna Grill:

1 (6 ounce) can tuna, drained and flaked
½ cup shredded Swiss cheese
½ cup diced celery
2 tablespoons onion, finely chopped
¼ cup mayonnaise
¼ cup sour cream
Dash pepper
8 slices rye bread
Pickles and olives for garnish

Combine all ingredients; mix well. Spread filling on 4 slices of rye bread. Top each with another slice of rye. Butter the outside of both slices. Grill in a frying pan or electric skillet until both sides are toasted and filling is heated through. Makes 4 sandwiches.

Rolled Cheese and Watercress:

1 (3 ounce) package cream cheese
1 teaspoon lemon juice
⅓ cup sour cream
½ teaspoon salt
1 teaspoon chives
1 cup watercress, chopped
18 slices white bread
3 tablespoon butter, softened
Parsley or watercress for garnish

Blend together cream cheese, lemon juice, sour cream, salt, chives and watercress. Trim crust from bread and roll slices with a rolling pin. Spread bread with butter, then the cheese mixture. Roll like a jelly roll. Chill. Slice each roll-up crosswise into 2 little rolls. Stand up on ends. Garnish. Makes about 36 sandwich rolls.

Frosted Triple Decker:

Sandwich bread
Chicken or tuna salad
Egg and olive salad
Cream cheese
Cream
Olives and parsley for garnish

Trim crust from sandwich bread. Butter one side. Spread chicken or tuna salad on one slice. Top with another slice of bread. On this, put egg and olive salad (add a few pimento stuffed olives, chopped, to egg salad) and top with a third slice of bread. Frost sides and top of sandwich with cream cheese that has been thinned with a little cream for spreading. Garnish. Give each guest a whole sandwich.

Champion Roast Beef:

8 slices dark rye bread
Butter, softened
½ cup sour cream
2 teaspoons dry onion soup mix
2 teaspoons prepared horseradish, drain
Dash freshly ground pepper
Thin slices cold roast beef
Lettuce

Spread bread slices with butter. Combine sour cream, onion soup mix, horseradish and pepper. Spread about 1 tablespoon of the sour cream mixture on each slice of bread. Top 4 slices with roast beef, then lettuce; cover with remaining bread. Makes 4 sandwiches.

Polly Jernigan
Opelika, Alabama

Author of Good! Good!! Good!!!
An excellent cookbook with selected recipes for party people.

TEA PARTY SANDWICHES

Too good to be left out

Avocado:

2 avocados, very ripe
2 hard-cooked eggs, grated
2 tablespoons lemon juice
1 teaspoon salt
2 dashes pepper
½ teaspoon curry powder
6 tablespoons mayonnaise

Mash avocados to a rough purée. Add remaining ingredients and blend thoroughly. Cover with plastic wrap and refrigerate. Makes 2 cups filling.

Chicken Salad:

2 cups minced, cooked chicken
1 cup finely chopped celery
1 cup finely chopped apples
5 tablespoons mayonnaise
1 tablespoon Durkee's sauce
½ teaspoon salt
¼ teaspoon white pepper
2 teaspoons lemon juice
¼ teaspoon onion powder

Combine chicken, celery and apples. Add remaining ingredients and blend thoroughly. Cover. May be refrigerated overnight. Makes 4 cups filling.

Egg Salad:

6 hard-cooked eggs, chopped
½ cup mayonnaise
2 teaspoons prepared mustard
2 or 3 ounces ripe olives, chopped
1 teaspoon salt
¼ teaspoon pepper

Combine all ingredients. Blend well. Cover. Refrigerate several hours. Makes 2 cups filling.

Cucumber Spread:

1 (8 ounce) package cream cheese, softened
1 large cucumber, peeled, seeded, grated and drained well
1 tablespoon onion, grated
2 tablespoons mayonnaise
¼ teaspoon lemon juice
Dash salt and pepper
Green food coloring (optional)
10 to 12 thin slices whole wheat bread, buttered
5 to 6 thin slices white bread, buttered

Combine all ingredients. Blend well. Spread on bread, using three slices for each sandwich. Wrap tightly in foil. Seal in plastic bag and freeze until needed. While slightly frozen, remove crust of bread from sandwiches. Slice thin into 4 finger size sandwiches; cut these in half, making 40 to 48 bite size canapés. Thaw completely before serving. Makes about 1½ cups filling. (I keep my freezer filled with these!)

Ham Salad:

1 cup ground cooked ham
3 tablespoons minced green pepper
2 tablespoons minced sweet pickles
2 teaspoons prepared mustard
4 tablespoons mayonnaise
2 tablespoons Durkee's sauce
2 tablespoons minced onions
1 hard-cooked egg, chopped
¼ teaspoon salt
¼ teaspoon pepper

Combine all ingredients. Blend well. Refrigerate several hours. Makes 1½ cups filling.

Olive and Nut:

2 (3 ounce) packages cream cheese
2 teaspoons lemon juice
1 teaspoon onion juice
¼ cup mayonnaise
1 (4½ ounce) can chopped ripe olives
½ cup pecans, finely chopped
Few dashes cayenne pepper
Seasoned salt to taste

Soften cream cheese; add other ingredients and blend well. Refrigerate. Makes 1½ cups filling.

Orange Marmalade Spread:

2 (3 ounce) packages cream cheese
4 tablespoons orange marmalade
¼ cup chopped pecan meats, toasted
½ teaspoon salt
½ teaspoon paprika

Soften cream cheese. Combine remaining ingredients with cheese and blend well. Spread on thin slices of buttered bread, crust removed, and cut into finger size sandwiches. Makes about 1 cup filling.

Peanut Butter and Chutney:

½ cup peanut butter
½ cup chutney, chopped fine
36 white bread rounds, toasted on both sides (1½ inch cutter)
Very small pieces of cooked, crisp bacon, if desired

Combine peanut butter and chutney. Spread mixture on toasted bread rounds. Bake in a preheated 400 degree oven for 5 minutes. Top with pieces of bacon. Serve hot. Makes 3 dozen.

Mushroom Rolls:

1 loaf thin sliced bread, crust removed
½ pound fresh mushrooms, finely chopped
¼ cup butter, melted
3 tablespoons flour
1 cup light cream
½ teaspoon salt
½ teaspoon onion salt
1 teaspoon lemon juice
3 or 4 tablespoons butter, softened

Roll bread slices very thin with rolling pin. Sauté mushrooms in butter for 5 minutes. Stir in flour until well blended. Add cream and cook until thickened, stirring constantly. Add salt, onion salt and lemon juice. Blend well, then cool. Place 1 to 2 teaspoons of mixture on each slice and roll up, seam side down. Butter top side of each roll. Freeze an hour or two; wrap in foil and return to freezer. When ready to serve, cut in thirds and bake in a preheated 400 degree oven for 10 minutes. Serve hot. Makes 2½ to 3 dozen.

PLAN AHEAD-BE PREPARED SANDWICHES

A freezer filled with ham and cheese . . . Good!

2 pounds shredded baked or boiled ham
½ pound Swiss cheese, sliced thin
20 to 24 soft buns
½ cup butter, softened
½ cup prepared mustard
1 tablespoon onion, dehydrated
1 tablespoon Worcestershire sauce
3 tablespoons poppy seed

Preheat oven to 275 degrees. Place ham and cheese on buns. Mix together butter, mustard, onion, Worcestershire sauce and poppy seed. Spread on buns. Wrap individually in foil. Freeze. To serve not frozen, bake in foil 20 to 25 minutes. To serve if frozen, bake in foil about 45 minutes.

Mary Tatham
Tequesta, Florida

CHEESE CRISP

- 2 cups avocado dip (page 21)
- 8 medium size tomatoes, fully ripe
- Salt
- 1 pound sharp Cheddar cheese
- 1 pound Monterey Jack cheese
- 1 large avocado
- Lime juice
- Oil for frying
- 8 flour tortillas
- Mexican green chilies and tomato sauce, hot

Make avocado dip and refrigerate. Peel, seed and finely chop tomatoes; lightly salt and place in colander to drain. Shred the cheese and blend together; cover and refrigerate. Slice avocado into thin slices, sprinkle with lime juice, cover and refrigerate. Thirty minutes before serving, heat 1 inch of oil in skillet. Fry tortillas over medium heat, turning 2 or 3 times with tongs. This will make them brown evenly and become crisp. Drain on paper towels. When all tortillas are cooked, place on cookie sheets and mound each one with cheese all over the top; use cheese generously. Place in preheated 350 degree oven until cheese melts.

To assemble: Place each tortilla on a serving plate, put a mound of avocado dip in the center and sprinkle tomatoes evenly over the cheese. Arrange 5 slices of avocado over tomatoes. Serve with green chilies and tomato sauce. Serves 8.

Cookie Smith
Vero Beach, Florida

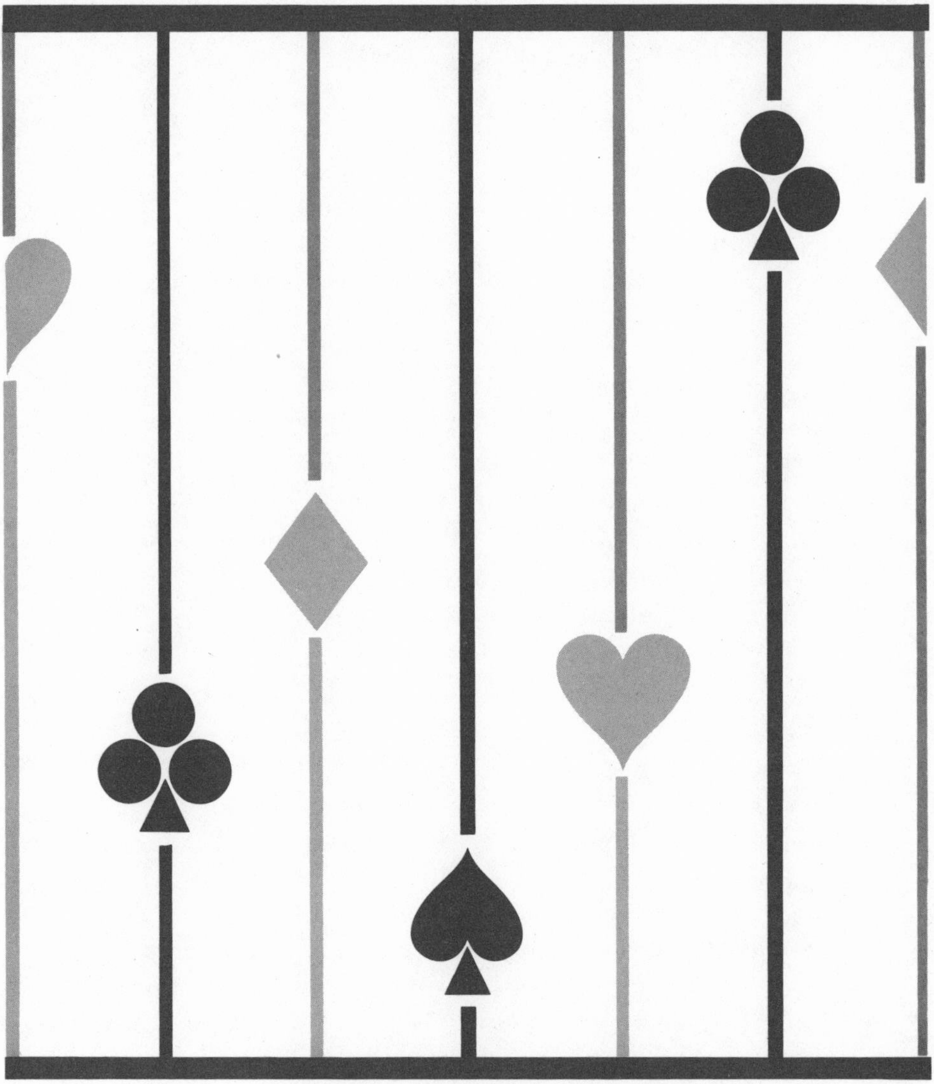

DESSERTS and SWEETS

BANANA CAKE

A big, beautiful birthday cake—a special request from my sons

1 cup butter
2½ cups sugar
4 eggs, beaten
4 to 5 bananas, sliced thin
4 cups cake flour
2 teaspoons baking powder
2 teaspoons soda
2 cups buttermilk
2 teaspoons vanilla extract

Cream butter and sugar with an electric beater; add eggs and bananas. Beat mixture thoroughly on low speed. Sift flour once; resift with baking powder and baking soda. Add flour to butter mixture alternately with the buttermilk, starting and ending with flour. Add vanilla. Pour batter into three greased layer cake pans. Place in a cold oven; set at 350 and bake 25 to 30 minutes. When cake is cool, cover each layer, top and sides, with icing.

Icing:

2 egg whites, unbeaten
1½ cups sugar
5 tablespoons cold water
¼ teaspoon cream of tartar
1½ teaspoons light corn syrup
1 teaspoon vanilla extract
Flaked coconut

In the top of a large double boiler place all ingredients but vanilla and coconut. Over rapidly boiling water, beat constantly with electric or rotary beater for 6 to 7 minutes. Remove from heat; add vanilla. Continue beating until icing is the right consistency to be spread. After cake is iced, sprinkle coconut on top and sides. Serves 14 to 16.

CHOCOLATE CAKE

There is no other!

1 cup butter
2 cups sugar
4 eggs
2 cups flour, sifted
¼ teaspoon salt
1½ teaspoons soda
⅔ cup buttermilk
1 teaspoon vanilla extract
3 (1 ounce) squares unsweetened chocolate, melted in ⅔ cup boiling water

Preheat oven to 325 degrees. Cream butter and sugar with electric beater until light and fluffy. Add eggs, one at a time, and beat well after each addition. Sift flour with salt. Mix soda with buttermilk and add alternately with flour to creamed mixture, starting and ending with flour. Add vanilla and melted chocolate with water; stir until smooth. Grease a 9x13-inch pan. Pour batter into pan and bake 50 to 55 minutes. Cool in the pan. While slightly warm, frost with chocolate frosting. Makes about 20 (2-inch) squares. The cake freezes well.

Chocolate Frosting:

½ cup margarine
1½ cups sugar
⅓ cup milk
¾ cup semi-sweet chocolate pieces
1 cup chopped pecans or walnuts (optional)

In a heavy saucepan cook margarine, sugar and milk to a full rolling boil. Boil for 2 minutes. Remove from heat; add chocolate pieces and nuts. Blend quickly. Beat until a spreading consistency. (It won't take more than a minute or two.) Spread at once over chocolate cake.

Betty Cole
Ludington, Michigan

FLOWER GARDEN CAKE

A delicate and delicious cake—pretty too

1 (10 inch) angel food cake
1½ envelopes unflavored gelatin, softened in ¼ cup cold water
6 eggs, separated
¾ cup sugar
¾ cup lemon juice
2 teaspoons grated lemon rind
Pinch salt
1 cup heavy cream, whipped
Maraschino cherries or nuts for garnish

In the top of a double boiler, combine slightly beaten egg yolks, sugar, lemon juice, lemon rind and salt. Cook over hot, not boiling water, until mixture coats a spoon. Remove from heat and stir in gelatin. Beat egg whites until stiff. Fold into custard. Tear angel food cake into small pieces. Add to the custard. Mix gently covering all pieces. Pour mixture into an oiled angel food cake pan. Chill until firm. Unmold and ice with whipped cream. Decorate with maraschino cherries or nuts. Serves 16.

Lillian Paxson
Vero Beach, Florida

OATMEAL CAKE

Cake is moist, freezes well—you'll eat every crumb!

½ cup margarine
1 cup raw quick-cooking oatmeal
1¼ cups boiling water
1 cup firmly packed brown sugar
1 cup white sugar
2 eggs, beaten
1½ cups flour
½ teaspoon salt
1 teaspoon soda
1 teaspoon cinnamon

Preheat oven to 375 degrees. Place one stick of margarine, oatmeal and boiling water in a bowl. Stir and set aside for 20 minutes. Combine all other ingredients. Add oatmeal mixture and blend thoroughly. Pour into a 9x12-inch pan. Bake 40 minutes.

Topping:

6 tablespoons melted butter
½ cup firmly packed brown sugar
¼ cup evaporated milk
¼ teaspoon vanilla
1 cup flaked coconut
½ cup chopped pecans

Mix all ingredients together and spread over the top of the cake when you take it from the oven. Place it under the broiler until it bubbles, but don't brown it.

Effie White
Goren Master Teacher
Mason, Texas

POP CORN CAKE

This is my most treasured recipe. It brings back many happy memories of Christmas. It was a family tradition to make this for our holiday parties. I thank my sons, Kim and Carey, for their help in the making and the *pounding*!

2 cups unpopped corn
Salt
1 cup black walnut meats
1 pint medium Orleans molasses
Butter, the size of a walnut
2 or 3 loaf pans, depending upon size, well greased

Pop corn. Add salt. Turn out into a large roasting pan or large dish pan. Add nuts and mix. Boil molasses until a soft ball in cold water (232-234). Add butter. Stir into pop corn quickly, covering all kernels. Pile mixture into loaf pans, pressing in with slightly wet hands. Pack down tightly and finish by pounding with a potato masher. Wrap in wax paper. Let stand overnight. To serve, slice down like a cake. A wonderful Christmas present . . . if you can give one away.

My Mother, Cherry Kindel Orr
Nashville, Tennessee

Dorothy Jane Orr Cook

THE BEST PRALINES

¾ cup butter
2 cups sugar
1 teaspoon soda
1 cup buttermilk
2 cups pecan halves
1 teaspoon vanilla extract

Cook butter, sugar, soda and buttermilk in a large, heavy pan. Cook to 240 degrees. Stir frequently. Remove from stove and with electric beater, beat for 5 minutes. Add pecans and vanilla. Continue beating by hand until mixture drops out easily on wax paper. Cool. Wrap individually in clear plastic. These keep indefinitely. Makes about 4 dozen.

Helen Corbitt
Dallas, Texas

DIVINITY FUDGE

Pick a dry day

2 cups sugar
½ cup light corn syrup
½ cup hot water
2 egg whites
⅛ teaspoon salt
1 teaspoon vanilla extract
1 cup pecans, chopped

In a heavy bottomed saucepan, place sugar, corn syrup and water; stir to dissolve sugar. Bring to a boil, without stirring, to 265 degrees on candy thermometer. Wipe sugar crystals away from sides of pan several times during cooking. While syrup is in last stages of boiling, beat egg whites and salt to stiff peaks. Pour hot syrup over egg whites in a fine stream, beating constantly with an electric beater. Continue beating until mixture beings to lose gloss and thickens. Fold in vanilla and pecans. Drop by teaspoonful onto wax paper. Makes 1 pound.

OUR FAVORITE CHOCOLATE FUDGE

4 (1 ounce) squares unsweetened chocolate
1½ cups milk
4 cups sugar
2 dashes salt
2 tablespoons corn syrup
4 tablespoons butter
2 teaspoons vanilla extract
1 cup broken pecans

In a large heavy saucepan add chocolate to milk and stir over low heat until smooth. Add sugar, salt and corn syrup; stir until mixture comes to a boil. Using a candy thermometer, cook to 234 degrees. Remove from heat, add butter and vanilla. Cool. Beat with electric beater until thick. Fold in pecans. Pour into a large buttered dish. Makes 2 pounds.

Kimberly Orr Cook
Redding, Connecticut

Carey Orr Cook
Menlo Park, California

Made for their grandfather, Carey Orr
Chicago, Illinois

CALIFORNIA BRITTLE

A great toffee
A happy project for the family

1 pound butter
2 cups sugar
6 tablespoons water
12 small Hershey bars (plain)
2 cups finely chopped pecans

Place butter, sugar and water in a large, heavy saucepan. Stir constantly to 300 degrees on candy thermometer. Remove from heat. Pour into a buttered 15½x10½-inch pan and spread thin. Spread the Hershey bars over mixture; add chopped pecans. Press pecans into the chocolate slightly with a sheet of wax paper. When cool, break into pieces. Store in airtight container. Makes 2 pounds.

Phyl Miller
Blowing Rock, North Carolina

CARAMEL APPLES

For my young friends

1 (14 ounce) bag caramels
2 tablespoons water
6 medium size apples

Melt caramels with water in the top of double boiler over low heat. Stir occasionally until mixture is smooth. Meanwhile remove stems from apples, then wash and wipe dry. Insert a wood stick in stem end of each apple making certain it is secure. Dip apples, one at a time, into hot caramel sauce; turn until coated. Scrap off excess sauce from bottom of apple. Place coated apples on greased wax paper and chill until firm. Serves 6.

TOFFEE SQUARES

1 cup butter
1 cup firmly packed brown sugar
1 egg yolk, beaten
2 cups flour, sifted
1 teaspoon vanilla extract
1 (8 ounce) sweet milk chocolate Hershey bar
½ cup pecans, chopped

Preheat oven to 350 degrees. In an electric mixer, cream butter and sugar until light; add egg yolk. Add flour blending well; add vanilla. Spread thinly on a 15½x10½-inch greased cookie sheet. Bake 15 to 17 minutes. Remove from oven. Break chocolate into squares and place on surface while warm. Spread over entire top. Sprinkle pecans over all, pressing in with a sheet of wax paper. Cut while warm. Makes 54 (1½-inch) squares.

Mi Mi Garnett
Evanston, Illinois

ALMOND MACAROONS

These are the best!

1 (8 ounce) can almond paste
1 cup sugar
⅛ teaspoon salt
2 tablespoons flour
⅓ cup confectioners' sugar, sifted
⅓ cup egg whites, unbeaten

Preheat oven to 325 degrees. Soften and crumble almond paste in a bowl. Work in gradually the sugar, salt, flour and confectioners' sugar; mix thoroughly. Add unbeaten egg whites and blend well. Drop by teaspoonful, 1 inch apart, on unglazed brown paper cut to fit cookie sheet. Bake 20 minutes or until light brown. Cool for 5 minutes. Remove by placing sheet of brown paper and cookies on a wet towel. Remove carefully. Makes 4 dozen.

Ina Edens
Tryon, North Carolina

FAMOUS PASTRIES OF VIENNA

Almond Squares

1 cup butter (no substitutes)
¾ cup sugar
1 egg, separated
½ cup almond paste
1 teaspoon almond extract
2 cups all-purpose flour, sifted
½ cup sliced or slivered almonds

Preheat oven to 350 degrees. Cream butter and sugar in a large bowl. Add egg yolk, almond paste and almond extract. Beat well; add flour and beat just until blended. Do not over-beat. Smooth with a spatula into an ungreased 11x7x1½-inch pan. Beat egg white until foamy and brush over surface of the dough. Scatter almonds over top. Bake 30 to 35 minutes. Cool and cut into squares. Makes about 3 dozen.

DELICATE LEMON SQUARES

Ever so good! I like these right out of the freezer

Crust:

1 cup butter, softened
2 cups flour, sifted
½ cup confectioners' sugar

Mix thoroughly by hand and press into a 13x9-inch pan. Bake for 15 to 20 minutes in a preheated 350 degree oven.

Filling:

4 eggs
2 cups sugar
6 tablespoons lemon juice
Grated rind of 1 lemon
1 tablespoon flour
½ teaspoon baking powder

Beat eggs slightly. Add sugar, lemon juice, rind, flour and baking powder. Mix together and pour on top of baked crust. Bake for 25 to 30 minutes. When cool, sprinkle with sifted confectioners' sugar. Makes 4 dozen.

Lil Dixson
Winston-Salem, North Carolina

MELTING MOMENT

The name says it all

½ cup butter, softened
2 tablespoons sugar
1 teaspoon vanilla extract
1 cup ground nut meats
1 cup cake flour, sifted
Confectioners' sugar

Preheat oven to 300 degrees. Cream butter and sugar until light and fluffy; add vanilla. Mix nuts with flour and add to butter mixture. Chill dough for ½ hour. Roll into balls or crescent shape. Bake on buttered cookie sheet for 25 to 30 minutes. When cool, sift confectioners' sugar over cookies. Store in a tin box. Makes about 3 dozen.

Bess Orr Cullen
Whitefish, Montana

QUAKERS' BEST

Oatmeal, of course

1½ sticks unsalted butter, softened
1⅓ cups firmly packed dark brown sugar
2 large eggs
1 teaspoon vanilla extract
1 cup flour, sifted
¾ teaspoon soda
½ teaspoon salt
¼ teaspoon nutmeg
2 cups old-fashioned Quaker Oats
1 cup dark, seedless raisins

Preheat oven to 350 degrees. Cream butter and sugar with an electric mixer. Beat until mixture is fluffy. Beat in eggs, one at a time, beating well after each addition; add vanilla. Into another bowl mix the flour, soda, salt and nutmeg; stir the mixture into the butter mixture, and add oatmeal and raisins. Drop the batter by the teaspoon, about 2 inches apart, onto a buttered baking sheet. Bake 12 minutes. Remove from oven, let cool for 1 minute, transfer to racks, and let them cool completely. May freeze. Makes 80 cookies.

Mary Lourie
Wilmette, Illinois
Wife of the former Chairman of the Board of the Quaker Oats Company

GUESS-AGAIN COOKIES

The crisp bits in these are potato chips!

1 cup butter, softened (no substitutes)
½ cup sugar
1½ cups flour
1 teaspoon vanilla extract
¾ cup finely crushed fresh potato chips

Preheat oven to 325 degrees. Mix butter and sugar in electric mixer until fluffy. Add flour and mix until smooth. By hand, add vanilla and potato chips; mix well. Drop on ungreased cookie sheet by small teaspoonfuls. Bake 15 to 20 minutes, until light brown. Cool and sprinkle with sifted confectioners' sugar. These freeze exceptionally well. Makes 5 dozen.

Alice Strom
Boynton Beach, Florida

FUDGE BROWNIES

For bridge players and brownies and boy scouts and baseball players and big boys too! The best!

1 cup butter
4 (1 ounce) squares chocolate, unsweetened
4 eggs, well beaten
2 cups sugar
1 cup flour, sifted
¼ teaspoon salt
2 teaspoons vanilla extract
1 to 1½ cups chopped pecans

Preheat oven to 350 degrees. Place butter and chocolate in top of double boiler and heat until melted. Remove and cool. Beat eggs and sugar with electric beater until blended. Add cooled chocolate mixture. Blend well. Add sifted flour, salt and vanilla. On low speed, mix thoroughly. Stir in pecans. Pour into a buttered 13x9-inch pan. Bake 30 minutes, or until a slight imprint will be left when top is touched lightly. Cool and cut into squares. Makes 4 dozen.

Mary Hollis Clark
San Diego, California

FORGOTTEN COOKIES

The young people won't let you forget!

2 egg whites
½ cup sugar
1 teaspoon vanilla extract
¾ cup chocolate chips *or* 1 cup pecan pieces

Preheat oven to 350 degrees. Beat egg whites until stiff, gradually adding sugar. Fold in vanilla and chocolate chips or pecans. Drop meringue batter, about ½ teaspoon at a time, onto an ungreased cookie sheet, an inch apart. Place in oven. Turn off heat and forget! . . . several hours or overnight. Store in a tightly closed container. Makes about 5 dozen.

Martha Wolfer
Cheyenne, Wyoming

FROSTED DELIGHTS

So good!

Crumb Layer:

½ cup butter, softened
½ cup firmly packed brown sugar
1 cup flour, sifted

Preheat oven to 350 degrees. Combine butter, sugar and flour and mix until the texture of coarse meal. Pat into a buttered 9x12-inch baking pan. Bake 10 to 12 minutes or until slightly brown.

Topping:

2 eggs, beaten
1 cup firmly packed brown sugar
2 tablespoons flour
½ teaspoon baking powder
½ teaspoon salt
1 teaspoon vanilla extract
1 to 1½ cups pecans, chopped

Combine all ingredients and spread evenly over partially baked crumb layer. Continue baking for 25 minutes. Cool.

Frosting:

1½ cups confectioners' sugar
1 to 2 tablespoons lemon juice

Combine frosting ingredients and spread over top. Makes 3½ dozen.

SCOTCH SHORTBREAD

Delicious—an authentic Scottish recipe

1 pound butter, softened
1 cup fine granulated sugar
5 cups flour, sifted

Preheat oven to 275 degrees. Cream butter and sugar. Gradually add flour blending thoroughly. Roll the dough out to ½ inch thick*; cut it into triangles or finger-sized strips. Place on buttered heavy baking sheets. Prick the dough all over with a fork in even rows and close together. Bake approximately 40 minutes or until bottoms are slightly browned. Cool the strips on racks. Makes 10 dozen.

*The shortbread may be rolled into balls; flatted with stoneware cookie stamp on baking sheet. The stamp embosses designs on cookies.

Barbara Morrison
Vero Beach, Florida

TEREZ'S COOKIES

Thin—crisp—delicious

1 cup butter, softened
1¾ cups sugar
¼ cup firmly packed brown sugar
2 eggs
3½ cups cake flour
2½ teaspoons baking powder
½ teaspoon salt
2 teaspoons vanilla extract
1 cup pecan pieces

Preheat oven to 350 degrees. Cream butter and sugar with electric beater; add eggs and mix well. Sift flour, baking powder and salt; add to butter-sugar mixture. Mix thoroughly. Add vanilla and pecan pieces. Chill the dough. When firm, form into three long rolls. Slice very thin. Bake on greased cookie sheet about 10 minutes. These rolls of dough may be frozen and baked as needed. Makes 6 dozen.

Hilda Hoffman
Washington, D. C.

WYOMING WAGON WHEELS

Moist and chewy

4 eggs
2 cups extra fine granulated sugar *or* sift granulated sugar
2 teaspoons vanilla extract
½ cup butter or margarine, melted
4 (1 ounce) squares chocolate, melted
2 cups flour, sifted
2 teaspoons baking powder
1 teaspoon salt
½ cup walnuts, chopped
Confectioners' sugar, sifted

Beat eggs with sugar and vanilla. Blend in butter and chocolate. Sift dry ingredients together; add to chocolate mixture and blend well. Add walnuts. Chill several hours or overnight. Shape into 1-inch balls, roll in confectioners' sugar and place on an ungreased cookie sheet about 1½ inches apart. Bake in a preheated 350 degree oven for 10 minutes. (Remove from the oven before they "look" done for a moist and chewy cookie). The balls expand into a wagon wheel pattern! Makes 80 cookies.

Martha Wolfer
Cheyenne, Wyoming

#1 SUGAR COOKIES

1 cup butter (no substitutes)
1 cup sugar
1 egg, beaten
1 teaspoon vanilla extract
2 cups and 2 tablespoons unsifted flour
½ teaspoon soda
½ teaspoon cream of tartar
Pinch of salt

Preheat oven to 350 degrees. Cream butter and sugar. Add eggs and vanilla and beat until fluffy. Sift the dry ingredients and combine with the butter and sugar mixture. Chill for 1 hour. Roll into small balls, dip in sugar and press thin with bottom of a glass. For the holidays, add red or green sprinkles. Do not butter cookie sheet. Bake 10 to 12 minutes. May freeze. Makes about 6 dozen.

SINFUL BROWNIES

These are so delectable they're worth a guilty conscience

1 (14 ounce) package soft caramels
½ cup evaporated milk
1 (6 ounce) package semi-sweet chocolate chips
1 (19 ounce) package Devil's Food Deluxe II cake mix
¾ cup butter, melted
⅓ cup evaporated milk

Preheat oven to 350 degrees. In the top of a double boiler melt caramels, evaporated milk and chocolate chips. To the cake mix add butter and evaporated milk; blend. Spread half of batter in a greased 9x13 inch aluminum pan. Bake 6-10 minutes. Remove from oven and spread melted caramel-chocolate mixture over cake. Top with remaining batter. At this point the batter will be difficult to spread. Bake 5 minutes; spread top batter more evenly. Return to oven and bake an additional 15-20 minutes. When cool, cut into squares. Note: Do not use a cake mix that has pudding in the mix. Makes 4 dozen.

Barbara Morrison
Vero Beach, Florida

GRAPES JUANITA

Lovely, light and good!

2 pounds white seedless grapes
1½ cups sour cream
½ cup firmly packed light brown sugar, maybe a little more
Grated orange rind, for garnish
1 strawberry for each serving

Wash, stem and dry grapes. Stir in sour cream and brown sugar. Chill for several hours or overnight. Add more sugar if needed. Serve in parfait glasses and garnish with orange rind and strawberries. Serves 8.

Muff Craven
Concord, North Carolina

FABULOUS HOT CHOCOLATE SOUFFLÉ

To prepare a dish for sweet soufflé, use a straight-sided oven-proof baker. Grease the bottom and sides well with butter. Dust the inside with confectioners' sugar.

2 tablespoons butter
1 tablespoon flour
1 cup milk
2 (1 ounce) squares unsweetened chocolate
⅓ cup sugar
3 eggs, separated
1 teaspoon vanilla extract
Whipped cream

Preheat oven to 350 degrees. Melt butter, add flour and stir 3 to 4 minutes. In the top of a double boiler, heat milk, chocolate and sugar until chocolate is melted; with hand beater, beat until smooth. Add the hot milk mixture to the flour mixture, stirring constantly until well blended. Beat egg yolks until light. Beat part of the sauce into the yolks, then add the yolk mixture to the rest of the sauce and stir the custard over low heat to permit the yolks to thicken. Remove from heat and cool well. Whip the egg whites until stiff but not dry. Add vanilla to custard; fold in egg whites. Pour into a 7-inch soufflé dish; set in a pan of hot water and bake about 30 minutes; test by inserting a silver knife part way into center of soufflé; if it comes out clean, soufflé is done. If any soufflé adheres to knife, bake 5 minutes more. Serve immediately with whipped cream. Serves 4.

BRANDY ALEXANDER

Nectareous!

4 ounces brandy
2½ ounces crème de cacao
6 to 7 scoops vanilla ice cream

Place in blender, about half at a time; blend a few seconds. Pour into chilled champagne or wine glasses. Serves 4.

FROZEN ALMOND BALLS WITH HOT FUDGE SAUCE

Your children will love you for this—guests too

Vanilla ice cream
Sliced toasted almonds
Hot fudge sauce

Make the ice cream balls using a scoop. Roll in sliced toasted almonds pressing ice cream against almonds. Balls hold their shape perfectly when wrapped individually in wax paper. Place in freezer until ready to serve. They may also be wrapped in foil and frozen.

Hot Fudge Sauce:

3 (1 ounce) squares unsweetened chocolate
1¾ cups light cream or half and half
1 cup sugar
¼ cup flour
¼ teaspoon salt
1 tablespoon butter
1 teaspoon vanilla extract

Melt chocolate in cream in top of double boiler over hot water. Cook until smooth, stirring occasionally. Combine sugar, flour, salt; add enough chocolate mixture to make a smooth paste. Add to remaining chocolate mixture. Cook until smooth and slightly thickened, about 10 minutes. Remove from heat and add butter and vanilla. The sauce keeps very well and may be served hot or cold.

Elizabeth Salter
Auburn, Alabama

HOT BRANDIED GRAPEFRUIT

A nice first course too

1 grapefruit
2 tablespoons dark brown sugar
1 teaspoon butter
1 tablespoon brandy

Halve grapefruit. Remove seeds with tip of a sharp knife. Cut around each section to loosen flesh from membrane and skin. Combine brown sugar, butter and brandy. Spread on top of grapefruit halves. Broil about 10 minutes, or until golden, or bake at 450 for 20 minutes. Serve at once. Serves 2.

COFFEE TORTONI

Good!

1 egg white
1 tablespoon instant coffee (not freeze dried)
⅛ teaspoon salt
⅓ cup sugar
1 cup heavy cream
1 teaspoon vanilla extract
⅛ teaspoon almond extract
¼ cup toasted almonds, chopped
Chocolate curls for garnish, optional

Combine egg white, coffee and salt in an electric mixer; beat until stiff. Add 2 tablespoons sugar, continue beating until satiny in texture. In a separate bowl, whip cream until it holds peaks, gradually add remaining sugar, vanilla and almond extract. Fold the egg white mixture into whipped cream mixture and add toasted almonds. Line a 6-cup muffin tin with paper muffin cups. Pour in mixture and freeze for at least 2 hours. Garnish with chocolate curls. Serves 6.

Betty Robinson
Kenilworth, Illinois

CHOCOLATE POTS DE CRÈME

A lovely dessert

½ cup sugar
3 tablespoons Droste cocoa
½ cup heavy cream
4 egg yolks, slightly beaten
Grated rind of 2 oranges (optional)

In a heavy saucepan combine sugar and cocoa; mix. Add heavy cream and bring to a boil. Remove from heat and stir in egg yolks. Return to low heat and cook, stirring constantly with a wooden spoon, until thickened. Stir in grated orange rind. Pour into 6 pots de crème cups and refrigerate until thoroughly chilled. Remove from refrigerator a few minutes before serving. Serves 6.

Melissa Beacom
Winnetka, Illinois

MACAROON BOMBE

Elegant party dessert

¾ cup sugar
1½ tablespoons flour
1 egg, slightly beaten
2 cups milk
1 (8 ounce) can crushed pineapple, drained
1 (10 ounce) jar maraschino cherries, chopped
2 cups crumbled almond macaroons
½ cup chopped pecans
2 cups heavy cream, whipped

In a heavy saucepan mix sugar and flour. Add egg and milk; mix thoroughly. Over medium heat, cook until thick, stirring constantly (15 to 20 minutes). Cool. Stir in fruit, cookie crumbs and nuts. Fold in whipped cream. Turn into a large refrigerated tray and freeze until firm. Serves 12.

MICKEY MOUSSE

Loved by all—the young and young at heart

1 quart vanilla ice cream
1 (8 or 9 ounce) container of Cool Whip
1 tablespoon instant coffee, diluted with 1 tablespoon water
5 (⅞ ounce) Heath bars, crushed (keep in freezer until ready to use)
1 package lady fingers, unfilled

Let ice cream soften a little. Mix in Cool Whip, coffee and crushed Heath bars, saving a handful to sprinkle on top. Line a 9x13-inch dish with lady fingers (opened) and pour ice cream mixture on top. Sprinkle with a handful of Heath bars. Put in freezer. Serves 10 to 12.

Rosamond Wilson
Fayetteville, New York

GRAND MARNIER CHOCOLATE MOUSSE

Ambrosial

1 (12 ounce) package semi-sweet chocolate bits
4 eggs
4 tablespoons Grand Marnier
1½ cups scalded milk

In the container of a blender, combine all ingredients. Blend at high speed for 2 minutes. Spoon into a crystal bowl or 8 dessert cups. Cover with plastic wrap and chill until ready to serve.

Topping:

1 cup heavy cream
2 teaspoons confectioners' sugar, sifted
1 teaspoon Grand Marnier
Grated chocolate for garnish (optional)

Whip the cream until stiff, gradually adding confectioners' sugar. Fold in Grand Marnier. Refrigerate. When ready to serve, garnish mousse with whipped cream and grated chocolate. Serves 8.

Cherry Jackson Sveen
Franklin, North Carolina

STRAWBERRY OR RASPBERRY MOUSSE

1 teaspoon unflavored gelatin
1 tablespoon liquid (fruit juice or water)
1 (10 ounce) package slightly sweetened strawberries or raspberries
2 cups whipping cream
½ cup confectioners' sugar, sifted
¼ teaspoon salt

Soften gelatin in liquid. Mash fruit to a pulp; add gelatin mixture. Combine cream, sugar and salt in a chilled bowl. Whip until stiff. Fold into fruit mixture. Turn into refrigerator tray; freeze 3 to 4 hours, or until firm. Serves 6.

PINEAPPLE SHERBET

1 (1 pound, 4 ounce) can crushed pineapple
¼ cup pineapple juice
½ cup water
¾ cup sugar
2 tablespoons lemon juice
1 cup whipping cream, whipped
2 egg whites, beaten stiff

Drain juice from pineapple; reserve ¼ cup. In a small saucepan cook pineapple juice, water and sugar for 10 minutes. Add pineapple and lemon juice. Cool. Pour into a refrigerator tray covered with foil and place in freezer until it has a slushy consistency (about 2 hours). Fold whipped cream and beaten egg whites into pineapple mixture. Pour into a 9x5-inch pan. Cover; return to freezer until firm. Remove from freezer to refrigerator about 20 minutes before serving. Serves 8.

NO SECONDS DESSERT—"BROWN SQUIRREL"

A fancy finale

12 scoops vanilla ice cream
2 ounces Amaretto di Saronno
1 ounce brandy

Mix in blender and refrigerate. Stir before pouring into chilled wine glasses, about ¾ full. Serve immediately. Serves 8.

Bebe Rand
Clayton, Missouri

PEACH CRUMBLE

Mighty good

8 sliced peaches, fresh or frozen
1 teaspoon lemon juice
1 cup flour, sifted
1 cup firmly packed dark brown sugar
⅛ teaspoon salt
½ cup butter
1 cup heavy cream, whipped

Preheat oven to 375 degrees. Arrange peaches in a buttered 1½-quart casserole; sprinkle with lemon juice. Mix together flour, sugar, salt; cut in butter until coarse as meal crumbs. Sprinkle crumb mixture over peaches. Bake 30 minutes. Serve hot and pass a dish of whipped cream. Serves 6.

PEACH PERFECTION

Delicious

3 cups very ripe peaches, mashed
2 cups sugar
¾ teaspoon Fruit-Fresh
3 cups peaches, cut into small pieces
1 package Sure-Jell

Thoroughly mash 3 cups peaches; add sugar and Fruit-Fresh. Mix well. Stir in 3 cups cut peaches and Sure-Jell. Fill 2 ice cube trays with mixture. Cover with foil; freeze. Remove from freezer a few minutes before serving. Delicious plain or may be served as a topping for ice cream. Serves 12.

Elizabeth Salter
Auburn, Alabama

GLAZED PECANS

4 cups pecan halves, unsalted
4 tablespoons light corn syrup
½ cup margarine, melted
Salt to taste

Preheat oven to 250 degrees. Combine pecans, corn syrup and melted margarine. Bake in a heavy skillet for 50 to 60 minutes. Stir occasionally to evenly glaze. Pour out on brown paper bags; separate pecans. Sprinkle lightly with salt. Store in air-tight container in refrigerator or freezer.

Betty Cole
Ludington, Michigan

SPICED SUGARED NUTS

1 cup sugar
5 tablespoons water
1 tablespoon powdered cinnamon
1 teaspoon vanilla extract
2 cups pecan halves

Bring to a boil the sugar, water, cinnamon and vanilla. When it is boiling merrily, add the pecans and let the whole come to a lively boil again. Remove from stove and stir constantly until the syrup starts to turn to sugar. Pour the whole out onto a lightly buttered cookie sheet and separate the nuts one from the other. Cool.

Kim and Carey Cook

PEANUT BUTTER PIE

*The young people will enjoy the making—
everyone will enjoy the eating*

1 (9 inch) baked pie crust
½ cup peanut butter
1 cup confectioners' sugar, sifted
1 (3 ounce) package cream cheese, softened
½ cup milk
1 (9 ounce) carton Cool Whip

Mix peanut butter, sugar, cream cheese and milk until well blended. Fold in Cool Whip. Pour into pie crust. Cover and freeze. Take out 30 minutes before serving. Serves 6.

Kirby Brown
Blowing Rock, North Carolina

SUPERB FUDGE PIE

It really is! and you'll like it served warm too

½ cup butter
3 (1 ounce) squares unsweetened baking chocolate
4 eggs, beaten
3 tablespoons white corn syrup
1½ cups sugar
¼ teaspoon salt
1 teaspoon vanilla extract
1 (9 inch) unbaked pie shell
Vanilla ice cream (optional)

Preheat oven to 350 degrees. In the top of a double boiler, melt butter and chocolate. Meanwhile, place eggs in mixing bowl and beat until light. Beat into the eggs the syrup, sugar, salt and vanilla. Stir in the chocolate mixture which has been slightly cooled; blend well. Pour into pie shell. Bake for 25 to 30 minutes, or until top is crusty and filling is set but somewhat soft inside. Do not over-bake. Pie should shake like custard so it will not be too stiff when cool. This may be served plain, but is best served with a topping of a thin spade of vanilla ice cream. Serves 8.

Hugh Parsley
Oxford, Mississippi

PERFECT PIE CRUST

Always tender, even with excess handling

4 cups flour
1 tablespoon sugar
2 teaspoons salt
1¾ cups Crisco, room temperature
½ cup water
1 tablespoon white or cider vinegar
1 large egg

Preheat oven to 450 degrees. In a large bowl mix flour, sugar and salt with a fork. Add Crisco; mix with a pastry blender or fork until crumbly. In a small bowl beat water, vinegar and egg; add to flour mixture and stir until moistened. Divide dough into 4 equal portions; shape each into a ball and chill for ½ hour or longer. Each ball makes one pie shell. Roll out on lightly floured surface; sprinkle a little flour on top of ball also. For a baked pie shell, place in a 9-inch pie pan, prick bottom and sides with fork. Bake 12 to 15 minutes. The balls can be frozen for several months. Defrost in refrigerator. Dough can be refrigerated several days. Makes 4 pie crusts.

Karen Brown
Vero Beach, Florida

Bobbi Shellen
Vero Beach, Florida

CHESS PIE

Very rich—your reputation as a cook is made!

½ cup butter
1½ cups sugar
1 tablespoon flour
1½ teaspoons white vinegar
1 teaspoon vanilla extract
3 whole eggs, beaten
1 (9 inch) unbaked pie shell

Preheat oven to 350 degrees. Melt butter; remove from heat. Mix sugar and flour together; add to melted butter with all other ingredients. Whisk thoroughly. Pour into pie crust. Bake 35 minutes, or until a knife inserted into the center comes out clean. Serves 6 to 8.

Lillian Paxson
Vero Beach, Florida

HEAVENLY CHOCOLATE PIE

I've said it all!

1 (8 inch) pastry shell, baked
½ cup slivered almonds, toasted
1 envelope unflavored gelatin
¼ cup cold water
½ cup unsweetened cocoa, sifted
1 cup confectioners' sugar, sifted
2 cups whipping cream
1 teaspoon vanilla extract
Additional whipped cream
Toasted almonds for garnish

Sprinkle the almonds over the bottom of the pastry shell. Set aside. Soften gelatin in cold water. Dissolve over hot water. Remove from heat. Combine cocoa, confectioners' sugar, whipping cream and vanilla. Beat until light and fluffy. Gradually add dissolved gelatin and continue beating until mixture forms stiff peaks. Turn into baked pastry shell. Refrigerate several hours before serving. Garnish with whipped cream and toasted almonds. Serves 6.

ALMOND PIE

Simply delicious

3 egg whites
¾ cup sugar
1 teaspoon almond flavoring
1 teaspoon baking powder
9 saltine crackers, crushed fine
1 cup chopped pecans
1 teaspoon butter, melted
Whipped cream

Preheat oven to 325 degrees. Beat egg whites until very stiff, slowly adding sugar; add almond flavoring and baking powder. Blend thoroughly. Fold in crushed crackers and pecans. Melt butter in a 9-inch pie plate; coat bottom and sides with butter. Add batter and bake for 25 minutes. Serve hot or cold with whipped cream. Serves 6.

Enda von Seeberg
Opelika, Alabama

STRAWBERRY MERINGUE PIE

Your best bridge-playing friends will put up with you! and go home happy

2 cups sugar
6 egg whites
1 teaspoon baking powder
¼ teaspoon salt
2 teaspoons vinegar
2 teaspoons water
2 teaspoons vanilla extract
1 quart fresh strawberries, sliced
2 cups whipping cream, whipped
2 to 3 tablespoons confectioners' sugar, sifted
1½ teaspoons vanilla
Whole strawberries, for garnish

Preheat oven to 275 degrees. Sift sugar. Set aside. With an electric beater, at high speed, beat egg whites, baking powder, salt, vinegar, water and 2 teaspoons vanilla until stiff. Continue beating and add sugar 1 tablespoon at a time. When all sugar has been added, continue beating for several minutes. Put batter in two 10-inch cake pans, with removable rims, that have been buttered and dusted lightly with flour. Bake about 1½ hours. Leave in the oven to cool. When the meringues are cool, place one on a serving platter. Place the strawberries on top; cover with the other meringue. Whip the cream until stiff. Fold in confectioners' sugar and vanilla. Cover the top and sides of the meringues with the whipped cream. Refrigerate several hours. Decorate with whole strawberries around bottom of platter. Serves 12.

SOUTHERN PECAN PIE

Seven testers said it was delicious!

1 cup sugar
½ cup white corn syrup
½ cup butter, melted
3 eggs, well beaten
1 cup pecan halves
1 (9 inch) unbaked pie shell

Preheat oven to 400 degrees. Mix sugar, syrup and butter. Add eggs. Place pecan halves in pie shell; add mixture. Bake at 400 degrees for 10 minutes. Reduce heat to 350 and continue baking for 30 to 35 minutes. Serves 6 to 8.

PUMPKIN PIE WITH GINGERSNAP CRUST

Something special

Crust:

1½ cups gingersnap crumbs
½ cup butter

Mix together and pack into sides and bottom of a 9-inch pie plate.

Filling:

1½ cups cooked, mashed pumpkin
1 cup firmly packed brown sugar
3 egg yolks
½ teaspoon salt
½ teaspoon ginger
¼ teaspoon allspice
2 teaspoons cinnamon
1 tablespoon gelatin
¼ cup cold water
3 egg whites, beaten
2 teaspoons sugar
1 cup whipping cream, whipped
Additional gingersnap crumbs

Combine pumpkin, brown sugar, egg yolks, salt, ginger, allspice and cinnamon. Cook in the top of a double boiler until consistency of custard. Remove from heat. Add gelatin dissolved in cold water. Cool. Fold in stiffly beaten egg whites to which sugar has been added. Turn into a crumb lined pie plate and chill until firm. To serve, top with whipped cream and additional crumbs. Serves 8.

NO CRUST COCONUT PIE

Makes two pies. Enjoy one, share one!

1¾ cups sugar
½ cup self-rising flour
4 eggs, well-beaten
¼ cup butter, melted
1 teaspoon vanilla extract
2 cups milk
7 to 8 ounces coconut (fresh or flaked)

Preheat oven to 350 degrees. Mix sugar and flour. Add beaten eggs, then remaining ingredients. Pour into two greased, 9-inch foil pie tins. Bake from 35 to 40 minutes, until brown on top. No crust is needed.

ANGEL PIE

Gorgeous looking and a heavenly taste

Meringue:

4 egg whites
¼ teaspoon cream of tartar
1 cup sugar
Pinch of salt
1 teaspoon vanilla extract

Preheat oven to 275 degrees. Beat egg whites until frothy. Add cream of tartar and beat until stiff, gradually adding sugar and salt. Fold in vanilla. Spread in a 9-inch buttered pie pan covering bottom and sides; shape with the back of a spoon, making the bottom ¼ inch thick and the sides 1 inch thick. Bake for 1 hour; leave in the oven to cool for 1 hour.

Filling:

4 egg yolks
½ cup sugar
¼ cup lemon juice
2 tablespoons grated lemon peel
2 cups whipping cream
Toasted almonds, for garnish

Beat egg yolks until lemon-colored, gradually adding sugar, lemon juice and lemon peel. Cook in the top of a double boiler over hot water (not touching pan) until thick, stirring constantly. This will take between 5 and 8 minutes. Cool. Fold in one cup of cream, whipped. Spread over meringue and cover with one cup of cream, whipped. Sprinkle toasted almonds over the top. Refrigerate a minimum of 12 hours. May be made the day before serving. Serves 8.

Hilda Hoffman
Washington, D. C.

TWO EXTRA FAVORITE DEALS
ONE GALLON OF BLOODY MARY MIX

Into a gallon jug put the following ingredients:

1 tablespoon celery salt
1 tablespoon salt
1 (5 ounce) bottle Worcestershire sauce
10 drops Tabasco
½ cup lemon juice
Fill to the top with V-8 juice

Shake well and refrigerate. For a large party, add 5 cups vodka to 1 gallon of mix.

Leila Stringer
Anderson, South Carolina

PLANTER'S PUNCH

It is a beautiful holiday drink . . . or any time

8 ounces orange juice
2 ounces light rum
1 ounce red grenadine syrup
1½ ounces dark rum
Sprig of mint for garnish

Combine orange juice and light rum; stir and add ice cubes. Add the grenadine syrup pouring it down the inside of the glass (it will layer on the bottom). Pour the dark rum slowly over the ice cubes; this will float on the top. Garnish with mint and serve with a straw. The drink may be made two hours ahead of serving.

Allen Marshall
Columbia, South Carolina

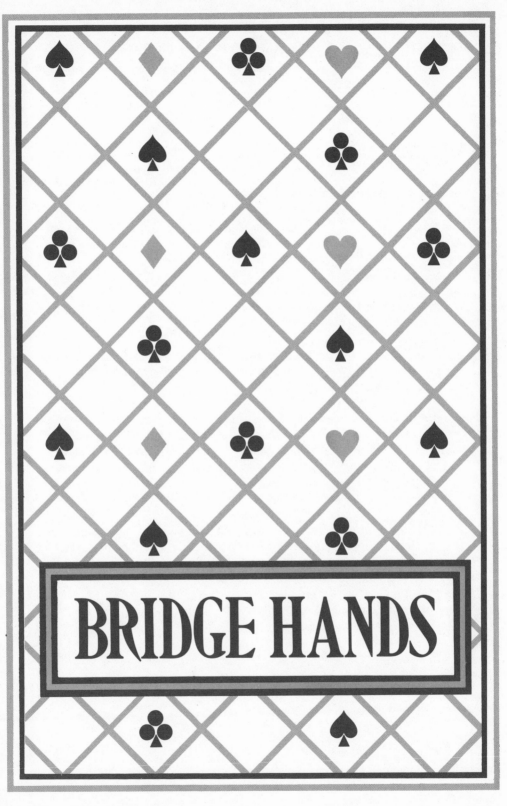

BRIDGE HANDS

THE EARLY PLAY AT SUIT AND NOTRUMP

Many times victory or defeat rests on decisions made by the declarer very early in the play of a hand.

The average player wins the first trick and then begins to think about the problem at hand. Frequently, it is too late! My advice is to slow down, hold your breath, count to something, but don't win the first trick until you know what you want to do at the second trick.

An experienced player studies the dummy after the opening lead has been made, gathers the clues available, the lead, the bidding, etc. He can forgive any dummy (partners frequently overbid); he is interested in only one thing—winning the number of tricks needed for his contract.

At notrump contracts, the declarer counts his sure tricks, decides which suit to attack to develop additional winners, and studies the entry situation.

At suit contracts, the declarer counts his losers. Frequently he can trump a loser in the dummy before drawing trump. There may be a long suit in the dummy which can be established to discard losers in the declarer's hand. Again, look for the entries; they may be the high trumps in the dummy.

The importance of extracting the opponents' trumps is not to be overlooked. If the declarer can see the number of tricks needed for his contract, he should lead trumps immediately. Leading trumps should be postponed when the trumps in the dummy are needed for ruffing purposes or needed as entries for a long side-suit to be developed to discard losers.

I hope you will be rewarded by studying the following lesson hands.

East dealer
Neither side vulnerable

Deal #1

North
♠ AQ106
♥ KQ105
♦ 74
♣ 543

West
♠ 54
♥ 86
♦ 108532
♣ QJ98

East
♠ 32
♥ AJ7432
♦ KQJ
♣ K10

South
♠ KJ987
♥ 9
♦ A96
♣ A762

East	**South**	**West**	**North**
1 Heart	1 Spade	Pass	3 Spades
Pass	4 Spades	Pass	Pass
Pass			

Opening lead: 8 of hearts

Declarer counts four losers: one heart, one diamond and two clubs. The club losers can be discarded on two high hearts if declarer makes the winning play of the five of hearts on the opening lead. East wins the jack and returns the diamond king, won by declarer's ace. The king and ace of spades are led. The king of hearts is played; if East covers with the ace, declarer trumps, gives up a diamond, and wins the club return with the ace. A diamond is trumped in the dummy and two clubs are discarded on the queen and ten of hearts. If East does not cover the king of hearts, declarer discards clubs. Makes four, losing one heart, one diamond and one club.

Mini-lesson: The overcall by South promises a five card suit, or longer, and a range of 10-15 points.

The jump raise of an overcall is not forcing. The bid shows about 12-13 points. When the overcall has been made at the one level, four card trump support should be held. With three card trump support, cue bid the opponent's suit and then raise partner's suit.

North dealer
North-South vulnerable

Deal #2

North
♠ AQ1094
♥ 8
♦ A3
♣ KQ1084

West
♠ 76
♥ A5
♦ KQJ85
♣ 7653

East
♠ 8532
♥ 7643
♦ 976
♣ A2

South
♠ KJ
♥ KQJ1092
♦ 1042
♣ J9

North	**East**	**South**	**West**
1 Spade	Pass	2 Hearts	Pass
3 Clubs	Pass	3 Hearts	Pass
4 Clubs	Pass	4 Hearts	Pass
Pass	Pass		

Opening lead: King of diamonds

Declarer allows the king of diamonds to win the first trick. If declarer wins the opening lead with the ace, there are four losers: one heart, two diamonds and one club. By allowing West to win the king of diamonds, South can trump a diamond in the dummy. If West shifts to a trump at trick two, a high one or a low one, declarer drives out the ace of hearts and still has control of the diamond suit. After pulling the remaining trumps, the declarer discards the losing diamond on a high spade in the dummy.

Mini-lesson: The bidding by North shows at least five spades and five clubs. With five clubs and four spades, North would open the bidding with one club.

The response by South, at the two level in a new suit, is forcing for one round and promises ten or more high card points.

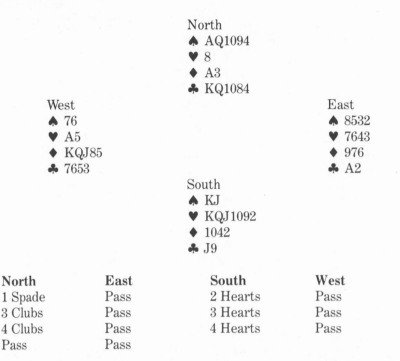

South dealer
East-West vulnerable

Deal #3

North
♠ K72
♥ 952
♦ 63
♣ A10932

West
♠ A106
♥ Q10843
♦ 8542
♣ 6

East
♠ 9854
♥ J6
♦ QJ109
♣ K74

South
♠ QJ3
♥ AK7
♦ AK7
♣ QJ85

South	**West**	**North**	**East**
1 Club	Pass	2 Clubs	Pass
3 Notrump	Pass	Pass	Pass

Opening lead: 4 of hearts

Declarer counts his winners: two hearts, two diamonds and four or five clubs, depending upon the position of the club king.

South wins the first trick with the king of hearts. A hold-up play, allowing East to win the jack, is dangerous; East may shift to a diamond, and declarer could be set, losing one spade, one heart, two diamonds and one club.

At trick two declarer leads the jack of spades. The only entry that West can have to establish his heart suit is the ace of spades. If West does not win his ace, declarer shifts to the clubs, taking the finesse, and although it loses, declarer has nine tricks and his contract. If West wins the ace of spades and continues hearts, South wins, takes the club finesse which loses, but East has no heart to return. If declarer improperly takes the club finesse at trick two and it loses, East returns a heart; if declarer ducks, West will force out the ace. When South leads a spade, West wins his ace, plus the good hearts, and the contract is defeated.

Mini-lesson: To raise one club to two, the responder needs four card support. The single raise shows 7-10 points and is a non-forcing bid.

South dealer
Both sides vulnerable

Deal #4

North
♠ Q1052
♥ AJ7
♦ 643
♣ Q74

West
♠ 874
♥ 10832
♦ K82
♣ 853

East
♠ 6
♥ K64
♦ J1097
♣ A10962

South
♠ AKJ93
♥ Q95
♦ AQ5
♣ KJ

South	**West**	**North**	**East**
1 Spade	Pass	2 Spades	Pass
4 Spades	Pass	Pass	Pass

Opening lead: 2 of hearts

The opening lead is won in the dummy with the ace. Declarer can lose one heart, one diamond and one club, but cannot afford to lose two diamonds. If South finesses the opening heart lead and the king is in the East hand, East may shift to a diamond.

Declarer leads three rounds of trump with the ace, king and ten. Clubs are led, forcing out the ace. East may cash the king of hearts and shift to a diamond; declarer takes the finesse of the queen which loses, but the other losing diamond can be discarded on the queen of clubs. Makes four, losing one heart, one diamond and one club.

Mini-lesson: Trump support for any suit, other than clubs, promises at least three trumps with an honor or four small. The single raise shows 7-10 points and is a non-forcing bid.

South dealer
Neither side vulnerable

Deal #5

North
♠ AQ104
♥ K8732
♦ K6
♣ 72

West
♠ 865
♥ 64
♦ QJ103
♣ J853

East
♠ KJ9
♥ Q
♦ A9852
♣ 10964

South
♠ 732
♥ AJ1095
♦ 74
♣ AKQ

South	**West**	**North**	**East**
1 Heart	Pass	3 Hearts	Pass
4 Hearts	Pass	Pass	Pass

Opening lead: Queen of diamonds

Declarer counts four possible losers: two spades and two diamonds. If the opening lead is covered with the king, East wins the ace, returns a diamond, West winning, and West returns a spade. South will go set, losing two spades and two diamonds.

The winning play is the six of diamonds at trick one. If West shifts to a spade, declarer wins with the ace, pulls the trumps and discards the losing diamond on the third high club. If West continues diamonds, East will be end played. Declarer wins the club shift by East at trick three, leads two rounds of trumps, cashes the remaining high clubs and leads a spade, finessing the ten. East wins the jack and must either lead a spade into dummy's ace-queen or lead a diamond or club which enables declarer to discard a spade loser as he trumps in the dummy. Makes four.

Mini-lesson: A jump raise by the responder shows 13-16 points, four trumps or more and is forcing to game.

If the responder has passed, a jump raise of partner's suit shows 11-12 points and is not forcing.

North dealer
East-West vulnerable

Deal #6

North
♠ AK42
♥ 94
♦ AQ732
♣ J2

West
♠ 53
♥ KQ10732
♦ K4
♣ AQ10

East
♠ 7
♥ J65
♦ J108
♣ 976543

South
♠ QJ10986
♥ A8
♦ 965
♣ K8

North	**East**	**South**	**West**
1 Diamond	Pass	1 Spade	2 Hearts
2 Spades	Pass	4 Spades	Pass
Pass	Pass		

Opening lead: King of hearts

Declarer counts five possible losers: one heart, two diamonds and two clubs.

West is allowed to win the first trick. This hold-up play by the declarer is made to avoid the possibility of East winning a heart trick and shifting to a club. Another danger exists in the diamond suit. If East has the king of diamonds, West surely has the ace-queen of clubs for his vulnerable overcall. Therefore, the diamond finesse must be successful in order to make the contract. Declarer wins the second heart lead and pulls trumps with the ace and queen. A low diamond is played, finessing the queen. A trump is led to declarer's jack and another diamond led; when West follows with the king, declarer plays low from the dummy. By this ducking play, East is kept out of the lead, and the dangerous club shift is avoided. Makes four, losing one heart, one diamond and one club.

Mini-lesson: A response at the one level in a new suit may have as few as six points, including high card points and distributional points, or as many as seventeen or eighteen points. The change of suit is forcing for one round.

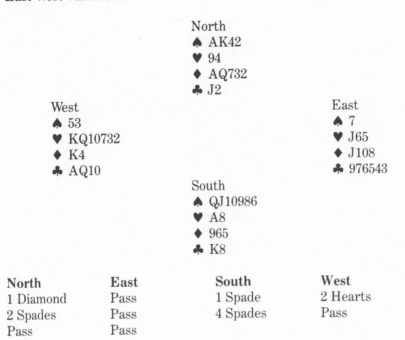

East dealer
North-South vulnerable

Deal #7

North
♠ A10954
♥ A8
♦ Q104
♣ K86

West
♠ 83
♥ Q54
♦ 7652
♣ J753

East
♠ 2
♥ KJ1063
♦ K983
♣ AQ10

South
♠ KQJ76
♥ 972
♦ AJ
♣ 942

East	**South**	**West**	**North**
1 Heart	1 Spade	Pass	4 Spades
Pass	Pass	Pass	

Opening lead: 4 of hearts

Declarer counts five possible losers: one heart, one diamond and three clubs. By allowing East to win the first heart, West may be unable to regain the lead for the dangerous club shift.

At trick two, East returns a heart won by dummy's ace. Declarer leads the king and ace of spades. A low diamond is led, and the jack is finessed, which wins. Declarer cashes the ace of diamonds, trumps a heart in the dummy, and leads the queen of diamonds, covered by the king, and declarer discards a losing club from his hand. East must either lead a club, which makes the king in the dummy a winner or lead a heart or a diamond, which allows declarer to discard a losing club as the dummy trumps. Makes four, losing one heart, one diamond and one club.

Mini-lesson: Holding three or more of your partner's suit headed by the king, queen, jack or ten, lead the lowest card. The underlined card is the proper lead: K72 Q953 J84 1052. Holding the ace of your partner's suit, always lead the ace against a suit contract.

Against a notrump contract, if you have three or more of your partner's suit headed by the ace, lead the lowest card.

North dealer
Both sides vulnerable

Deal #8

North
♠ KQ8
♥ AQJ107
♦ J2
♣ A85

West
♠ 7652
♥ 842
♦ K1073
♣ 104

East
♠ 1094
♥ K6
♦ Q965
♣ KQJ9

South
♠ AJ3
♥ 953
♦ A84
♣ 7632

North	East	South	West
1 Heart	Pass	1 Notrump	Pass
2 Notrump	Pass	3 Notrump	Pass
Pass	Pass		

Opening lead: 3 of diamonds

Declarer counts six winning tricks. The heart suit will develop the additional tricks needed for game. By analyzing the opening lead, and using the rule of eleven, declarer knows that the diamonds are divided evenly; West has four and East has four. Declarer wins the opening lead with the ace and takes the heart finesse, which loses to East. The defense can win three diamond tricks, and the declarer claims the balance of tricks. Makes three. The danger of a hold-up play at trick one, allowing East to win the queen of diamonds, is that a club shift may be made; this will defeat the contract. The defense will win one heart, one diamond and three clubs.

Mini-lesson: A one notrump response to an opening bid of one in a suit shows 6-10 high card points and is a non-forcing bid. It is not the cheapest response; a new suit bid at the one level is not only cheaper but more descriptive.

The Rule of Eleven is an exact mathematical calculation applicable whenever the card led is the leader's fourth highest of a suit. Here is the way it works: Subtract the denomination (number) of the card led from eleven; the result gives the number of *higher* cards than the one led in the other three hands. Counting the cards in his own hand and in the dummy which are higher than the one led, both declarer and the leader's partner can determine the number of such cards in the concealed hand of the other.

REBIDS BY OPENER

The rebid by the opener is probably the most important of all bids. The opening bid of one in a suit does not pretend to clarify the strength of the hand held by the opener. Such a bid may be made on as few as 13 points or as many as 20 to 23 points. It is the opener's second bid, after his partner's response, that will help clarify the precise strength and type of distribution. This will enable the partnership to determine how high to play and where to play.

The opener's hand will fall within the following four classifications:

A minimum hand (13 to 16 points)

With hands in this minimum range, you may or may not elect to bid again, unless partner's response to your opening bid is forcing.

A good hand (16 to 19 points)

You should make a constructive rebid. Avoid making any rebid which your partner might construe as discouraging.

A very good hand (19 to 21 points)

You should make a jump rebid in notrump, jump in your own suit or jump in partner's suit.

The powerhouse hand (21 points and up)

You should make a jump shift rebid which describes the strength of the hand and is forcing to game.

You will note that the upper limit of each classification coincides with the lower limit of the next higher classification. Point count cannot do everything. The true count of any hand is not really established until the bidding is over. A king, worth 3 points, can be rendered worthless one bid later. The decision on these "judgment points" should be made as the bidding progresses.

South dealer
East-West vulnerable

Deal #9

North
♠ KQJ6
♥ Q43
♦ A108
♣ 973

West
♠ 10987432
♥ 6
♦ J
♣ K1084

East
♠ 5
♥ 9872
♦ K75432
♣ J5

South
♠ A
♥ AKJ105
♦ Q96
♣ AQ62

South	**West**	**North**	**East**
1 Heart	Pass	1 Spade	Pass
3 Clubs	Pass	4 Hearts	Pass
4 Spades	Pass	5 Diamonds	Pass
6 Hearts	Pass	Pass	Pass

Opening lead: Jack of diamonds

Declarer counts three possible losers, one diamond and two clubs; however, the three high spades in the dummy will provide discards for the club losers.

The ace of diamonds wins the first trick as declarer follows suit with the queen. Four rounds of trumps are led, the ace of spades cashed and the six of diamonds led to the eight. If East takes the king, the ten of diamonds is an entry for the high spades; if East ducks the eight of diamonds, spades are led, discarding three club losers. Makes six.

Mini-lesson: The jump shift by the opener after a one level response shows about 21 points or more. The bid is forcing to game. With equal length in partner's suits, the responder is obligated to return to the first suit bid by partner. North, who has promised only 6 points with his response at the one level, jumps in the heart suit to show good values.

After the trump suit is agreed upon and the required number of points are held by the partnership to be in the slam zone, cue bidding may be used to show aces. The four spade bid by South shows the ace; the five diamond bid by North shows the ace.

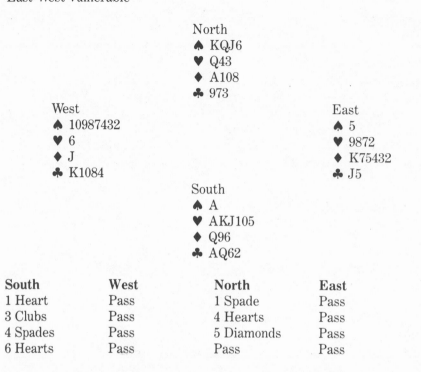

South dealer
Both sides vulnerable

Deal #10

North
♠ QJ1092
♥ 43
♦ 643
♣ KJ6

West
♠ 863
♥ Q872
♦ J7
♣ Q1084

East
♠ AK7
♥ 1096
♦ Q1098
♣ 732

South
♠ 54
♥ AKJ5
♦ AK52
♣ A95

South	**West**	**North**	**East**
1 Heart	Pass	1 Spade	Pass
2 Notrump	Pass	3 Notrump	Pass
Pass	Pass		

Opening lead: 4 of clubs

Declarer counts six winners: two hearts, two diamonds and two clubs. By giving the defense the ace and king of spades, South can develop three additional tricks. Using the rule of eleven, declarer counts three clubs in the dummy higher than the four and three in his own hand higher. Therefore, East has only one club higher than the one led.

The six of clubs is played from the dummy, covered by the seven and won by declarer's ace. This play gives declarer two entries to the dummy, the king and jack of clubs. South leads a spade at trick two, and East ducks. A second spade is led and the king wins. East returns the ten of diamonds which South wins. A club is led to the jack and another spade played driving out the ace. Declarer wins any return by East and the king of clubs is the entry to cash the high spades in the dummy. Makes four.

If South does not win the first trick with the ace of clubs, East can defeat the contract by refusing to win the first spade lead.

Mini-lesson: The 2 notrump jump rebid by the opener, after a response in a new suit at the one level, shows a balanced hand, the unbid suits protected and 19-20 high card points. The bid is highly invitational but not forcing.

South dealer — Deal #11
Neither side vulnerable

North
♠ K109
♥ A853
♦ 863
♣ Q92

West
♠ 654
♥ KQ109
♦ AQ105
♣ 108

East
♠ 32
♥ J762
♦ KJ
♣ 76543

South
♠ AQJ87
♥ 4
♦ 9742
♣ AKJ

South	West	North	East
1 Spade	Pass	2 Spades	Pass
3 Spades	Pass	4 Spades	Pass
Pass	Pass		

Opening lead: King of hearts

Declarer counts four losing diamonds in his hand; however, the dummy has only three diamond losers. There are no other losing tricks in the North hand; the three low hearts can be trumped by South.

The opening lead is won with the ace. Dummy's three hearts are trumped in declarer's hand with the ace, queen and jack of spades, retaining the seven and eight as entries to the dummy to continue the ruffing. The jack of clubs is overtaken with the queen; the king of spades takes the remaining trump from West as declarer discards one of his losing diamonds. Makes four, winning in all six spade tricks, one heart and three clubs.

Mini-lesson: The play on this hand is called a dummy reversal. There are two requirements: the dummy's trumps must be good enough to draw the adverse trumps; the declarer's hand must have a short suit.

East dealer
North-South vulnerable

Deal #12

North
♠ QJ9
♥ KJ2
♦ J1074
♣ 754

West
♠ 83
♥ A743
♦ Q963
♣ 986

East
♠ K7
♥ Q1098
♦ 852
♣ KQJ2

South
♠ A106542
♥ 65
♦ AK
♣ A103

East	**South**	**West**	**North**
Pass	1 Spade	Pass	2 Spades
Pass	4 Spades	Pass	Pass
Pass			

Opening lead: 9 of clubs

West elected to lead the "top of nothing." Declarer counts his losers: one possible spade, one or two hearts and two clubs. The spade finesse must win, for there are three sure losers, one heart and two clubs.

The jack of clubs is won with the ace. At trick two, declarer leads a heart, West plays low, and the king is played from the dummy. The reason for this play is that East is known to hold the king, queen and jack of clubs from the opening lead; the king of spades has to be in the East hand for the contract to be made. East, having passed as the dealer, is unlikely to have the ace of hearts; that would give him thirteen high card points and an opening bid. Makes four.

Mini-lesson: After a raise from partner, the opener revalues his hand if it contains a long trump suit. The following adjustment is in order:

Add 1 point for the fifth trump
Add 2 additional points for the sixth and each subsequent trump

North dealer
Both sides vulnerable

Deal #13

North
♠ K52
♥ K8
♦ J73
♣ AQ1086

West
♠ J106
♥ Q73
♦ KQ1092
♣ 74

East
♠ AQ87
♥ 105
♦ 8654
♣ 953

South
♠ 943
♥ AJ9642
♦ A
♣ KJ2

North	**East**	**South**	**West**
1 Club	Pass	1 Heart	Pass
1 Notrump	Pass	3 Hearts	Pass
4 Hearts	Pass	Pass	Pass

Opening lead: King of diamonds

Declarer counts four possible losers: three spades and one heart. By giving a heart trick to East, the declarer avoids the dangerous spade shift by West.

The ace of diamonds wins the opening lead. Declarer leads a low heart, West follows with the three, the eight is played from the dummy and East wins the ten. The diamond return is trumped by South. A heart is led to the king, a diamond trumped, and the ace of hearts draws the remaining trump. Two spades are discarded on the long club suit in the dummy. Makes five.

Mini-lesson: The one notrump rebid by the opener indicates a minimum and balanced hand.

Any jump by the responder, if not a passed hand, is forcing to game.

North dealer
Neither side vulnerable

Deal #14

North
♠ AQ
♥ 7653
♦ AQ
♣ AK1098

West
♠ KJ762
♥ 108
♦ 10753
♣ 62

East
♠ 1053
♥ 2
♦ KJ984
♣ Q543

South
♠ 984
♥ AKQJ94
♦ 62
♣ J7

North	**East**	**South**	**West**
1 Club	Pass	1 Heart	Pass
4 Hearts	Pass	4 Notrump	Pass
5 Spades	Pass	6 Hearts	Pass
Pass	Pass		

Opening lead: 3 of diamonds

There are two possible losers, one spade and one diamond; however, neither the spade finesse nor the diamond finesse is needed. Declarer can discard two spades and one diamond on the club suit.

The ace of diamonds wins the opening lead. Trumps are drawn in two rounds. Declarer cashes the ace and king of clubs and plays the ten of clubs. If East plays low, declarer discards his losing diamond. This play is called a Banker's Finesse . . . it costs nothing! If West wins the queen of clubs, South later discards two spades on the two remaining clubs. If East covers with the queen, declarer trumps high; he now leads the four of hearts to the seven and discards one diamond and one spade on the two high clubs in the dummy. The queen of diamonds is trumped, and the spade finesse taken. Makes seven.

Mini-lesson: The jump to game by North promises four or more trumps and about 20 points. South, with a rebid valuation of 15 points, (one for the fifth trump and two for the sixth trump), knows that the partnership is in the slam zone and uses the Blackwood Convention to ask for aces.

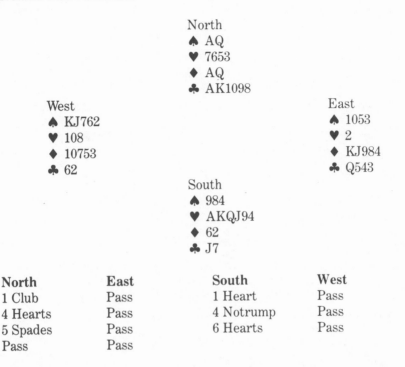

North dealer
North-South vulnerable

Deal #15

North
♠ AK102
♥ Q4
♦ AJ752
♣ K6

West
♠ QJ5
♥ J1092
♦ 109
♣ Q843

East
♠ 8
♥ K763
♦ 864
♣ AJ1075

South
♠ 97643
♥ A85
♦ KQ3
♣ 92

North	**East**	**South**	**West**
1 Diamond	Pass	1 Spade	Pass
3 Spades	Pass	4 Spades	Pass
Pass	Pass		

Opening lead: Jack of hearts

Declarer counts four possible losers: one spade, one heart and two clubs. If West is not allowed to regain the lead, the declarer can discard one or two clubs on the diamond suit.

The jack of hearts is covered with the queen; East follows with the king, and South plays low. East returns a heart, and declarer wins the ace. A low spade is led; West plays low, and the ten is played from the dummy. If the ten loses to an honor in the East hand, the ace and king will pick up the outstanding trumps. Declarer pulls the remaining trumps and discards both clubs on the long diamonds in the dummy. Makes six.

If South makes the error of winning the ace of hearts at trick one and loses a trump trick to East (he could have held the jack or queen of spades), East will return a heart which West wins. A club lead by West then sets the contract.

Mini-lesson: The jump by North promises four or more trumps, a good hand with 16-19 points (an average of 17 or 18 points), and is not forcing after a response at the one level.

South Dealer
East-West vulnerable

Deal #16

North
♠ A109
♥ 654
♦ Q10
♣ KQJ104

West
♠ 876
♥ K1083
♦ A84
♣ 852

East
♠ K432
♥ QJ97
♦ 763
♣ 93

South
♠ QJ5
♥ A2
♦ KJ952
♣ A76

South	**West**	**North**	**East**
1 Diamond	Pass	2 Clubs	Pass
2 Notrump	Pass	3 Notrump	Pass
Pass	Pass		

Opening lead: 3 of hearts

Declarer counts seven winners: one spade, one heart and five clubs. The additional tricks needed for game can come from the diamond suit after giving the opponents the ace, or from a successful finesse in the spade suit.

The clue to declarer's choice is the opening lead. Using the rule of eleven, South knows that the hearts are divided four-four in the opponents' hands.

The winning play is to give up the diamond ace immediately. East and West can win their ace and three heart tricks; declarer claims the balance, making three notrump.

If the spade finesse is taken, the defense will win one spade, three hearts and the ace of diamonds, setting the contract.

Mini-lesson: The 2 notrump rebid by the opener, after a response in a new suit at the two level, shows a minimum of 15 high card points, a balanced hand and the unbid suits protected. The bid is forcing to game except where responder makes a simple rebid of his own suit over 2 notrump.

South dealer — Deal #17

Neither side vulnerable

North
♠ 832
♥ K107
♦ Q3
♣ AK843

West
♠ Q1074
♥ Q43
♦ 974
♣ J106

East
♠ KJ95
♥ A65
♦ 8652
♣ Q7

South
♠ A6
♥ J982
♦ AKJ10
♣ 952

South	**West**	**North**	**East**
1 Diamond	Pass	2 Clubs	Pass
2 Diamonds*	Pass	3 Diamonds	Pass
3 Notrump	Pass	Pass	Pass

Opening lead: 4 of spades

Declarer counts seven winners: one spade, four diamonds and two clubs. There is no reason to hold-up the ace of spades. Using the rule of eleven, the declarer knows that the outstanding spades are divided four-four in the opponents' hands.

At trick two, declarer leads the nine of hearts, West plays low, dummy follows with the seven, and East may or may not win his ace. If he does not, the finesse is repeated. East and West can win three spade tricks, and declarer claims the balance. Makes three.

Leading the ace and king of clubs and giving up a club will set declarer, for the defense can score three spades, the ace of hearts and one club.

Mini-lesson: *Goren says, "It is better to mislead partner about your suit than to mislead him about the strength of your hand." A 2 notrump rebid by declarer would indicate a holding of 15-17 high card points. Put a heart in your diamond suit and rebid it. Don't admit that you did it.

North dealer
North-South vulnerable

Deal #18

North
♠ K643
♥ K7
♦ AQ853
♣ 83

West
♠ Q9
♥ 1083
♦ J107
♣ Q9762

East
♠ A1075
♥ J964
♦ K9
♣ J104

South
♠ J82
♥ AQ52
♦ 642
♣ AK5

North	**East**	**South**	**West**
1 Diamond	Pass	1 Heart	Pass
1 Spade	Pass	2 Notrump	Pass
3 Notrump	Pass	Pass	Pass

Opening lead: 6 of clubs

Declarer counts six winners: three hearts, one diamond and two clubs. The diamond suit may develop the additional tricks needed for game.

South wins the ten of clubs with the king. The normal play in diamonds is to duck one round and take the finesse of the queen on the second round. However, declarer can improve his chances immeasurably by learning the art of leading towards the closed hand.

At trick two, declarer leads a heart to the king and plays the three of diamonds. Depending upon the experience and caliber of the players in the game, South will win four diamond tricks if East plays the king. He will probably go set if East doesn't hesitate and then plays low. There is nothing to lose by the play. Against a large percentage of the players, declarer will make his contract.

Mini-lesson: The opener always shows a biddable four card major suit on his rebid, if he can do so at the one level.

North dealer
East-West vulnerable

Deal #19

North
♠ QJ82
♥ AJ62
♦ K2
♣ 862

West
♠ 73
♥ KQ1097
♦ Q87
♣ K95

East
♠ 4
♥ 854
♦ J10965
♣ J1074

South
♠ AK10965
♥ 3
♦ A43
♣ AQ3

North	**East**	**South**	**West**
Pass	Pass	1 Spade	Pass
3 Spades	Pass	6 Spades	Pass
Pass	Pass		

Opening lead: King of hearts

Delcarer counts two possible losers; however, the jack of hearts will end play West, who will be forced to lead a club into the ace-queen or give declarer a sluff and a ruff.

The ace of hearts wins the opening lead. A low heart is trumped with the nine. A low spade is led to the eight, and another heart is trumped with the ten. The ace of spades takes the outstanding trump away from West. Declarer leads a diamond to the king, a diamond back to the ace, and the losing diamond is trumped in the dummy. The jack of hearts is led, South discards the three of clubs, and West is end played. If West leads a heart, it will be trumped in the dummy as declarer discards the queen of clubs; if West elects to lead a club, the loser in that suit is eliminated. Makes six.

Mini-lesson: The jump raise by North, after he has passed, promises four or more trumps, about 11-12 points, and is not forcing.

South has 22 points, adding 1 point for the fifth trump and 2 points for the sixth trump. The combined count puts the partnership in the slam zone.

North dealer
Both sides vulnerable

Deal #20

North
♠ Q109
♥ KJ932
♦ AK
♣ 853

West
♠ 652
♥ 74
♦ J9752
♣ KQJ

East
♠ 3
♥ Q106
♦ 108643
♣ 10942

South
♠ AKJ874
♥ A85
♦ Q
♣ A76

North	**East**	**South**	**West**
1 Heart	Pass	2 Spades	Pass
3 Spades	Pass	4 Notrump	Pass
5 Diamonds	Pass	5 Notrump	Pass
6 Hearts	Pass	6 Spades	Pass
Pass	Pass		

Opening lead: King of clubs

Declarer counts three possible losers: one heart and two clubs. The high diamond in the dummy will take care of one loser.

The ace of clubs wins the first trick. Two rounds of trumps are led with the ace and king. The queen of diamonds is won in the dummy with the king; the ace of diamonds discards a heart. Declarer leads a heart to the ace, a heart to the king and trumps a heart high. South plays a trump to the queen and discards two clubs on the long heart suit. Makes seven.

Mini-lesson: When the opener has a choice of rebidding his own suit or of supporting his partner's suit, he usually should raise partner's suit.

The jump shift by the responder is forcing to game and strongly suggests a slam. The bid shows about 19 points or more. If the responder has a solid suit of his own or very good trump support for his partner, he may jump shift with 17 points.

THE FINESSE

The finesse is the first play learned by a beginning bridge player as a method of increasing the number of tricks he may be able to win. It is an elementary play and a very important play; the greatest of experts use finesses. Mathematically speaking, a finesse is a 50-50 proposition; it will be successful 50% of the time. Unless there is a better play available, the finesse stands to gain everything and lose nothing.

The beginner loves to take finesses; he is happy with a 50% chance of success. The expert's first choice is not the finesse. He is on the alert for a line of play that offers a better chance of success. Frequently the bidding will yield a clue as to the possible success or failure of an intended finesse. The skillful player will be able to locate cards from this bidding information or from discards of the opponents during the play.

A line of play which is frequently available to the declarer is the end play. This is a play taking place toward the end of the hand, usually at the tenth or eleventh trick. The preparation for an end play may begin as early as the first or second trick. It is an advanced technique with which declarer frequently can produce one additional trick. This is done by forcing the defenders to lead a key suit which presents declarer with a trick he might not make on his own.

Another line of play is the safety play. A safety play is exactly what its name implies: it is a play made to reduce to a minimum the risk of losing the contract. It is a method of protecting against a bad break. The expert will make any play that will give a modicum of safety to his contract. He will sacrifice one trick in order to run the least possible risk of losing two tricks; thus a finesse may be refused and a trick given up to avoid the loss of an additional trick if the finesse should fail.

There are necessary finesses and unnecessary finesses; the winning player will learn to distinguish between them.

North dealer
Neither side vulnerable

Deal #21

North
♠ Q6
♥ AJ82
♦ AK64
♣ K104

West
♠ KJ95
♥ 5
♦ QJ108
♣ Q832

East
♠ 108432
♥ 43
♦ 972
♣ 765

South
♠ A7
♥ KQ10976
♦ 53
♣ AJ9

North	**East**	**South**	**West**
1 Notrump	Pass	3 Hearts	Pass
4 Diamonds*	Pass	4 Notrump	Pass
5 Hearts	Pass	6 Hearts	Pass
Pass	Pass		

Opening lead: Queen of diamonds

Declarer counts two possible losers: one spade and one club There is no need to guess which way to finesse for the queen of clubs. There is an end play available which will force the opponents to lead a club, or lead another suit, which will give the declarer a sluff and a ruff. The king of diamonds wins the opening lead. Declarer cashes the king and queen of trumps and leads a diamond to the ace. A diamond is trumped, the dummy re-entered with a heart and the last diamond is trumped. Declarer leads the ace of spades and exits with a spade. West must either lead a spade, on which a club is discarded from either hand and trumped in the other, or make a club lead, which eliminates the guess in that suit. Makes six.

Mini-lesson: The one notrump opening is made with a balanced hand, 16-17-18 high card points, and at least three suits are protected. Any jump by the responder is forcing to game.

*The four diamond bid by North is called a feature bid. The bid shows a good fit for partner's suit, a near-maximum notrump opening and controls in the suit bid. It is the same as raising partner's suit and pinpoints outside strength.

South dealer
North-South vulnerable

Deal #22

North
♠ AJ1085
♥ A3
♦ A64
♣ K42

West
♠ 743
♥ KQJ84
♦ Q5
♣ J85

East
♠ void
♥ 109652
♦ 10983
♣ Q1076

South
♠ KQ962
♥ 7
♦ KJ72
♣ A93

South	West	North	East
1 Spade	Pass	3 Clubs	Pass
3 Diamonds	Pass	3 Spades	Pass
4 Notrump	Pass	5 Spades	Pass
6 Spades	Pass	Pass	Pass

Opening lead: King of hearts

Declarer counts two possible losers: one diamond and one club. The diamond suit may set up for a club discard.

The ace of hearts takes the first trick. Declarer leads three rounds of trump and trumps a heart. A safety play is made in the diamond suit. The king of diamonds is led and a low diamond led to the ace; when the queen falls, declarer loses one club. If the queen of diamonds does not fall, declarer will win the ace and a low diamond will be played towards the jack. If East has the queen, the losing club in the dummy will be discarded on the jack. If West has the queen, the club loser will be discarded on the fourth diamond in declarer's hand. If West has four diamonds to the queen, the contract cannot be made. Makes six.

Mini-lesson: The North hand is too strong for a jump raise in partner's suit. This bid is limited to 13-16 points. The responder makes a temporizing bid and supports spades on his next bid. The jump shift may be made with 17 points and very good trump support for partner's suit.

North dealer
East-West vulnerable

Deal #23

North
♠ 7
♥ KJ2
♦ AQ765
♣ Q853

West
♠ Q1084
♥ 83
♦ KJ103
♣ K97

East
♠ KJ6
♥ 765
♦ 942
♣ AJ104

South
♠ A9532
♥ AQ1094
♦ 8
♣ 62

North	**East**	**South**	**West**
1 Diamond	Pass	1 Spade	Pass
2 Clubs	Pass	2 Hearts	Pass
2 Notrump*	Pass	3 Hearts	Pass
4 Hearts	Pass	Pass	Pass

Opening lead: 3 of hearts

When planning a crossruff, the declarer will find it easier to count his winners. South counts nine winning tricks: one spade, five hearts in the South hand, two hearts in the North hand by trumping spades and one diamond. The diamond finesse must be successful to win ten tricks.
Declarer wins the trump lead with the nine and at trick two he leads a diamond, finessing the queen. The ace of diamonds is played and declarer trumps a diamond. The ace of spades is cashed and the crossruff proceeds, trumping spades in the dummy and diamonds in declarer's hand. Makes four. With any lead but a trump, the diamond finesse is not needed. There are ten winners: five hearts in the South hand, three hearts in the North hand, by ruffing spades, and two aces.

Mini-lesson: With two five card suits, South bids the higher ranking suit first and rebids the lower ranking.

*To raise partner's second bid suit at your first opportunity, four card trump support is needed.

The trump lead is proper when the bidding has indicated that the dummy has a short suit. The bidding by North indicates a shortness in his partner's first bid suit, spades. Another time when the trump lead is recommended is on a hand in which any other lead may be beneficial to the declarer.

South dealer
Both sides vulnerable

Deal #24

North
♠ 653
♥ A653
♦ AJ73
♣ 83

West
♠ AJ8
♥ 9
♦ 10862
♣ J10965

East
♠ Q1092
♥ Q107
♦ 94
♣ K742

South
♠ K74
♥ KJ842
♦ KQ5
♣ AQ

South	**West**	**North**	**East**
1 Heart	Pass	2 Hearts	Pass
4 Hearts	Pass	Pass	Pass

Opening lead: Jack of clubs

Declarer counts four possible losers: three spades and one heart. If South can keep the East player from gaining the lead, the dangerous spade shift will be avoided.

After winning the opening lead with the ace, South plays a low heart to the ace and returns a heart. When East follows with the ten, declarer plays the jack; if this loses, declarer makes four, losing two spades and one heart. When the finesse wins, declarer makes his game with an overtrick.

Mini-lesson: A one notrump opening is never made with a five card major suit and 18 high card points.

North dealer
North-South vulnerable

Deal #25

North
♠ Q1085
♥ J632
♦ A2
♣ AQ2

West
♠ 64
♥ A97
♦ J1097
♣ J764

East
♠ J2
♥ K108
♦ 6543
♣ K983

South
♠ AK973
♥ Q54
♦ KQ8
♣ 105

North	**East**	**South**	**West**
1 Club	Pass	1 Spade	Pass
2 Spades	Pass	4 Spades	Pass
Pass	Pass		

Opening lead: Jack of diamonds

Declarer counts four possible losers: three hearts and one club. After winning the opening diamond lead with the ace, South pulls trumps with the ace and king, cashes the king and queen of diamonds, discarding the two of clubs from dummy. A club is led to the ace and the queen of clubs is given to the defenders. After winning the king of clubs, East is end-played. If East elects to lead a heart, only two tricks will be lost in that suit; if he leads a diamond or a club, declarer will discard a heart from his hand as he trumps in the dummy. Makes four.

Mini-lesson: A bid of one club may be used to open the bidding holding only three clubs headed by an honor. The reason for this opening is that occasionally a hand is dealt where you have the required count to open the bidding, but there is no biddable suit; or you hold only one four card biddable suit and will have no convenient rebid should partner change suits. The one club bid is not forcing; pass if you hold fewer than six points.

South dealer
East-West vulnerable

Deal #26

North
♠ Q42
♥ AQJ86
♦ 64
♣ Q76

West
♠ 75
♥ K1092
♦ A107
♣ J1098

East
♠ 963
♥ 73
♦ KJ852
♣ K52

South
♠ AKJ108
♥ 54
♦ Q93
♣ A43

South	**West**	**North**	**East**
1 Spade	Pass	2 Hearts	Pass
2 Spades	Pass	3 Spades	Pass
4 Spades	Pass	Pass	Pass

Opening lead: Jack of clubs

Declarer counts five possible losers: one heart, two diamonds and two clubs. In order to make the contract, the heart finesse must win. On the opening lead the queen of clubs is played, covered by the king, and South wins the ace. At trick two, a heart is led, West plays low and the finesse of the jack wins. A spade is led to the king and another heart played finessing the queen. A low heart is trumped by declarer.* South cashes the ace of spades and leads a spade to the queen. Declarer discards two losing diamonds or two losing clubs on the ace of hearts and the fifth heart. Makes four.

Mini-lesson: The response of two hearts over a one spade opening promises a five card or longer suit. With only four hearts, the responder with nine other cards in his hand will have other bids available.

*This is an important play—only four heart tricks are needed.

6 cards outstanding will be divided:	3-3	36% of the time
	4-2	48% of the time
	5-1	15% of the time
	6-0	1% of the time

North dealer
Both sides vulnerable

Deal #27

North
♠ K1053
♥ A2
♦ A43
♣ Q865

West
♠ 74
♥ 9843
♦ KQ107
♣ K72

East
♠ 2
♥ J765
♦ 9652
♣ 10943

South
♠ AQJ986
♥ KQ10
♦ J8
♣ AJ

North	**East**	**South**	**West**
1 Club	Pass	2 Spades	Pass
3 Spades	Pass	4 Notrump	Pass
5 Hearts	Pass	6 Spades	Pass
Pass	Pass		

Opening lead: King of diamonds

Declarer counts two possible losers: one diamond and one club. The opening diamond lead is won with the ace. Two rounds of trumps are led and then three rounds of hearts, discarding a diamond from the dummy. South gives the jack of diamonds to West who is end-played. West has three choices—all losers—a heart or a diamond lead will be trumped in the dummy as declarer discards his losing club (this is called a ruff and sluff); if West leads a club, the loser in that suit is eliminated. Makes six, losing one diamond.

Mini-lesson: The finesse in the club suit is a 50% play; half the time the jack will win and half the time it will lose; the endplay is a 100% play.

North dealer
East-West vulnerable

Deal #28

North
♠ AQ82
♥ 652
♦ AJ
♣ KJ63

West
♠ 5
♥ A1073
♦ KQ1074
♣ 952

East
♠ 103
♥ QJ9
♦ 98532
♣ Q108

South
♠ KJ9764
♥ K84
♦ 6
♣ A74

North	**East**	**South**	**West**
1 Club	Pass	1 Spade	Pass
2 Spades	Pass	4 Spades	Pass
Pass	Pass		

Opening lead: King of diamonds

Declarer counts four possible losers: three hearts and one club. The king of diamonds is won with the ace. Declarer leads two rounds of trumps with the ace and king. The ace and king of clubs are played and the jack of diamonds led, on which South discards his losing club. This play will guarantee the game contract with any combination of cards which may be held by East and West.

1. On the actual hand: If West leads a club, dummy covers whatever is led; East follows with the queen and declarer trumps. South will discard one losing heart on the thirteenth club in the dummy.

2. If West has four clubs, and leads that suit, the jack in the dummy will be a winner and provide a discard for a losing heart.

3. If West has no clubs, he must lead a heart, which makes the king in declarer's hand a winner, or lead a diamond which will be trumped in the dummy as declarer discards a losing heart.

Mini-lesson: The opener holding four spades and four clubs, bids the club suit first.

LEADS, SIGNALS AND DEFENSE

Most experts agree that defensive play is the most difficult phase of bridge. The object of the defending side is the same as the object of the declarer; to win as many tricks as possible. The intitial lead is of paramount importance in the defenders' opening campaign to defeat the declarer. If chosen properly, the opening lead gives the defense crucial timing and frequently will spell the difference between victory and defeat. There is a great scope for judgment in the choice of this lead. To judge well, the defenders with an ear to the bidding have the advantage of knowing something about the declarer's hand. Also, there are fundamental principles available; these consist of a system of conventional leads and a system of signals. With the application of these principles, the defenders convey to each other the proper defense.

Whether the final contract is in a suit or in notrump, if the partner of the opening leader has bid a suit, it is generally best to lead that suit. When partner has not bid a suit, the lead of an unbid suit is best.

Hands should be classified; a chosen lead may be a proper one against a notrump contract but an improper one against a suit contract. Against a notrump contract it is essential to develop winning tricks out of low cards, to establish your suit before the declarer establishes his suit. Therefore, your longest suit usually should be selected as the opening lead.

When defending against a contract, the defenders must rely on a system of signals in order to be successful. Information that is needed for the defense of the hand can be given by the size of the cards that are played on various tricks. The play of an unnecessarily high card indicates strength in the suit or a desire to have that suit led or continued; a low card indicates weakness in the suit. This is called the Attitude Signal and generally is used when following to your partner's lead or when making a discard.

Another necessary signal is the Count Signal and usually is applied when following to a lead by the declarer. It is a method by which a defender can indicate to his partner the length held in a particular suit. With an even number of cards play high-low; with an odd number of cards play the lowest.

Basic defense starts with an ear to the bidding, signals by partner, inferences drawn from the play, and the number of tricks that can be counted for the declarer.

East dealer
Both sides vulnerable

Deal #29

North
♠ 985
♥ AQ4
♦ Q2
♣ Q10963

West
♠ 74
♥ 876532
♦ 1064
♣ 72

East
♠ AQ32
♥ 9
♦ KJ93
♣ A854

South
♠ KJ106
♥ KJ10
♦ A875
♣ KJ

East	**South**	**West**	**North**
1 Diamond	1 Notrump	Pass	3 Notrump
Pass	Pass	Pass	

Opening lead: 4 of diamonds

The overcall of 1 notrump by South shows the same values as an original 1 notrump opening bid. The notrump bidder must have the opponent's suit stopped.

West makes the proper lead of a low card of partner's suit holding three to the ten. The deuce is played from the dummy, East follows with the jack and declarer wins the ace. At trick two declarer leads the king of clubs, East winning with the ace. The king of diamonds smothers the queen; a low diamond is led to partner's ten. West returns a spade which East wins with the ace and the nine of diamonds is the setting trick. Down one.

Many beginning players will make the improper lead of the ten of diamonds, the top of partner's suit; declarer will cover with the queen, East follows with the king and the ace wins. Declarer now has an additional stopper with the eight and will lose only two diamond tricks and two aces, making his contract.

Mini-lesson: The opener, holding three four-card biddable suits, bids the suit below the singleton.

Leading partner's suit . . . review Deal #7.

North dealer
Neither side vulnerable

Deal #30

North
♠ 95
♥ KQ74
♦ 104
♣ AK1074

West
♠ A8
♥ 9832
♦ AK9832
♣ 8

East
♠ 743
♥ 65
♦ QJ7
♣ J9652

South
♠ KQJ1062
♥ AJ10
♦ 65
♣ Q3

North	**East**	**South**	**West**
1 Club	Pass	1 Spade	2 Diamonds
Pass	Pass	3 Spades	Pass
4 Spades	Pass	Pass	Pass

Opening lead: King of diamonds

Good defense by East and West will set South in an otherwise ironclad contract. Declarer counts three losers: one spade and two diamonds. The king of diamonds wins the first trick as East follows with the queen. At trick two, West leads the eight of clubs, South winning with the queen. The queen of trumps is led, West wins with the ace and returns the two of diamonds for East to win with the jack. East returns a club which West trumps, setting the contract one trick.

Mini-lesson: The queen is never used as a high-low signal. Therefore, if the defender follows suit with the queen on his partner's lead of the king, the defender either has a singleton or the jack of the suit led. It is an accepted convention that when the suit is continued, the leader must underlead his ace; partner will win the trick either with the jack or by trumping.

South dealer
North-South vulnerable

Deal #31

North
♠ QJ2
♥ 874
♦ 92
♣ AK952

West
♠ 1086
♥ A105
♦ Q1053
♣ 1064

East
♠ 97
♥ J962
♦ AK76
♣ QJ8

South
♠ AK543
♥ KQ3
♦ J84
♣ 73

South	**West**	**North**	**East**
1 Spade	Pass	2 Clubs	Pass
2 Spades	Pass	3 Spades	Pass
4 Spades	Pass	Pass	Pass

Opening lead: 3 of diamonds

Declarer counts four possible losers: two hearts and two diamonds. If the heart ace is in the East hand, the contract is assured. If not, South will play for the outstanding clubs to be divided three-three. Only two rounds of trumps will be led, the clubs tested and the queen of spades retained in the dummy as an entry to the good clubs.

However, East has other plans. Using the rule of eleven, East knows that South has three diamonds higher than the opening lead. By forcing the dummy to ruff a diamond at trick three, the entry for the club suit is eliminated. This good defense sets the hand. Down one.

Mini-lesson: The South hand revalues to 15 points.

Adding for length when partner raises your suit . . . Review Deal #12.

The rule of eleven . . . Review Deal #8.

North dealer
East-West vulnerable

Deal #32

North
♠ A92
♥ AK
♦ AK5
♣ J6532

West
♠ K65
♥ 964
♦ J83
♣ AQ108

East
♠ J1087
♥ 72
♦ Q1094
♣ K94

South
♠ Q43
♥ QJ10853
♦ 762
♣ 7

North	**East**	**South**	**West**
1 Club	Pass	1 Heart	Pass
2 Notrump	Pass	3 Hearts	Pass
4 Hearts	Pass	Pass	Pass

Opening lead: 4 of hearts

Declarer counts four possible losers: two spades, one diamond and one club. If the king of spades is in the East hand, the contract is assured. An additional chance is to develop a winner in the club suit. If the clubs do not break favorably, the spade play for the king in East's hand is still available.

The opening trump lead is won with the king. At trick two, a low club is led, won by West with the eight. Another trump is led, won by the ace and a second round of clubs played, declarer trumping with the ten. The queen of hearts takes the remaining trump from West. South plays a diamond to the king and a third round of clubs is trumped. A diamond back to the ace and the fourth round of clubs is trumped. The dummy is entered with the ace of spades and the diamond loser in declarer's hand is discarded on the thirteenth club. Makes four, losing two spades and one club.

Mini-lesson: East will have the king of spades 50% of the time. The outstanding seven clubs held by East and West will be divided as follows:

4-3	62%
5-2	31%
6-1	6½%
7-0	½%

South dealer
Neither side vulnerable

Deal #33

North
♠ AKQ73
♥ 52
♦ 863
♣ 852

West
♠ J2
♥ 943
♦ K1042
♣ KJ76

East
♠ 10986
♥ 106
♦ J975
♣ 1094

South
♠ 54
♥ AKQJ87
♦ AQ
♣ AQ3

South	**West**	**North**	**East**
2 Hearts	Pass	2 Spades	Pass
3 Hearts	Pass	4 Hearts	Pass
4 Notrump	Pass	5 Diamonds	Pass
5 Notrump	Pass	6 Diamonds	Pass
6 Hearts	Pass	Pass	Pass

Opening lead: 3 of hearts

Declarer has three potential losers: one diamond and two clubs; but on the other hand he has eleven sure winners.

When the dummy has a long suit that cannot be established by ruffing due to lack of entries, and there is no ruffing to be done in the dummy, declarer should count winners as if the hand were being played at notrump. With six heart winners and two minor suit aces, declarer needs four spade tricks, not five!

Declarer draws the trumps and ducks a spade, East winning. South wins the club return with the ace, runs the trumps and cashes four spade winners, discarding a diamond and two clubs. Makes six. If the spades don't break 4-2 (percentage is that they will), declarer can fall back on the diamond finesse.

Mini-lesson: Playing strong two bids, the opening two demand bid is forcing to game. The opener must have four quick tricks and be within one trick of game in his own hand.

North dealer
North-South vulnerable

Deal #34

North
♠ A32
♥ 5
♦ 8754
♣ AKJ92

West
♠ 106
♥ A74
♦ AKQJ3
♣ Q53

East
♠ J8754
♥ 983
♦ 102
♣ 864

South
♠ KQ9
♥ KQJ1062
♦ 96
♣ 107

North	**East**	**South**	**West**
1 Club	Pass	1 Heart	2 Diamonds
Pass	Pass	4 Hearts	Pass
Pass	Pass		

Opening lead: King of diamonds

Excellent defense will set the game contract, although at first glance it looks as though declarer will only lose one heart and two diamonds. On the king and queen of diamonds East follows with the ten and then the two; this is called an echo. West in analyzing the defense, and with an ear to the bidding, cannot figure to win anything in the spade suit or the club suit. Certainly declarer has strength in spades, having jumped to game. He does not have any points in the diamond or club suits. He does not have either major suit ace. If there is a future for the defense, it has to be in a trump promotion. At trick three, West leads the three of diamonds, East trumps with the eight of hearts, overtrumped by the ten. When declarer plays the king of hearts (it would be smart of South to lead the queen of hearts hoping West might duck), West wins the ace and returns a fourth diamond, trumped by East with the nine, overtrumped with the jack—and the setting trick is the seven of hearts! Down one.

Mini-lesson: This trump promotion play is called an uppercut. The play consists of using otherwise useless trumps on partner's lead, in order to force out declarer's high trumps; in so doing you promote a trump trick for partner.

East dealer
East-West vulnerable

Deal #35

North
♠ A108
♥ J73
♦ AQJ8
♣ 642

West
♠ void
♥ AK854
♦ 10942
♣ A1093

East
♠ 74
♥ Q10962
♦ K73
♣ QJ7

South
♠ KQJ96532
♥ void
♦ 65
♣ K85

East	**South**	**West**	**North**
Pass	4 Spades	Pass	Pass
Pass			

Opening lead: King of hearts

Declarer counts four possible losers: one diamond and three clubs. On the opening lead of the king of hearts, South makes the winning play of discarding the five of diamonds. With this play, South can keep East from gaining the lead and the dangerous club shift will be avoided. West continues with a heart which is trumped by South. Two rounds of spades are led and the ace and queen of diamonds played. If East doesn't play the king of diamonds, South discards a losing club. This play is the Banker's Finesse . . . it costs nothing. If East plays the king, South trumps and leads a spade to the dummy and discards a club on the good jack of diamonds. If West has the king of diamonds, he will win the queen with the king as declarer discards a losing club; however, the king of clubs is safe from attack. Declarer can discard another club loser on the jack of diamonds or score his king of clubs if West leads that suit. Makes four.

Mini-lesson: Pre-emptive bids are not made with good hands. They are relatively weak in high cards and contain a very long trump suit. The bid is an attempt to keep the opponents out of the bidding for the pre-emptive bidder has little, if any, defensive strength. The pre-emptive bidder should be prepared, if doubled, to lose no more than 500 points. If not vulnerable, he may overbid by three tricks; if vulnerable, he may overbid by two tricks. Because of the favorable location of key cards, East and West can make 6 hearts!

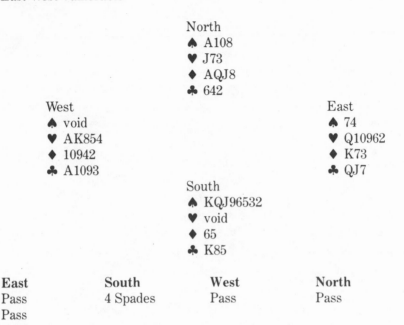

West dealer
Both sides vulnerable

Deal #36

North
♠ AQ10
♥ J1087
♦ 76
♣ AJ108

West
♠ 842
♥ 54
♦ AKJ1052
♣ K4

East
♠ 7653
♥ A9
♦ Q843
♣ Q96

South
♠ KJ9
♥ KQ632
♦ 9
♣ 7532

West	**North**	**East**	**South**
1 Diamond	Double	3 Diamonds	4 Hearts
Pass	Pass	Pass	

Opening lead: King of diamonds

Declarer counts one heart loser, one diamond loser and should lose only one club by a finesse of the ten and later finessing the jack. On this hand, when the king of club falls on the second lead of the suit, the finesse is not necessary. However, West had a plan for the defense; after winning the king of diamonds, he led the king of clubs. Declarer won the ace and played the jack of trumps, hoping that East might duck—thinking there was a finesse position. East stepped up with the ace, cashed the queen of clubs and returned a club which West trumped. This good defense set the contract one trick.

Mini-lesson: The double by North is a take-out double. A double in order to be a take-out, must be at the doubler's first opportunity to bid. It is a conventional bid asking partner to name his best suit. The doubler has an opening bid (13 points and up), and either support for the other three suits, two suits, one of which is a good five card suit, or a strong six card suit with a very good hand. The jump raise by East over the double is called a "barricade bid." The bid shows at least four trumps and about 8 to 10 points in support of partner's suit. It is not a forcing bid. Holding 10 high card points or more, with or without support for partner's suit, East would redouble.

North dealer
North-South vulnerable

Deal #37

North
♠ 54
♥ 95
♦ QJ10864
♣ AKQ

West
♠ Q10863
♥ KJ63
♦ K3
♣ 107

East
♠ J92
♥ A1074
♦ 72
♣ 6432

South
♠ AK7
♥ Q82
♦ A95
♣ J985

North	**East**	**South**	**West**
1 Diamond	Pass	2 Notrump	Pass
3 Notrump	Pass	Pass	Pass

Opening lead: 6 of spades

Declarer counts seven winners. If the diamond finesse is successful, South will win twelve tricks. When the diamond finesse loses to West, good defense will set the contract.

The king of spades wins the first trick. Declarer leads a club to the queen and returns the queen of diamonds, won by West with the king. West can count ten tricks for the declarer: two spades, five diamonds and three clubs. The only hope for the defense is in the heart suit. West leads the three of hearts* which East wins with the ace. East returns the four and the defense wins four heart tricks and one diamond to set the contract.

Mini-lesson: *When a defender switches suits (West led a spade on his opening lead and now has switched to the heart suit) . . . he wants his second suit led back if he leads a low card in his second suit; but he wants his first suit returned if he leads a high card in his second suit.

The jump to two notrump by the responder shows a balanced hand, 13-15 high card points and the unbid suits protected. The bid is forcing to game. If the responder has passed, the jump to two notrump shows 11-12 high card points and is not forcing.

South dealer
East-West vulnerable

Deal #38

North
♠ 82
♥ 94
♦ J10963
♣ K1098

West
♠ K1063
♥ Q8763
♦ A8
♣ 54

East
♠ AJ74
♥ 1052
♦ 754
♣ 632

South
♠ Q95
♥ AKJ
♦ KQ2
♣ AQJ7

South	**West**	**North**	**East**
2 Notrump	Pass	3 Notrump	Pass
Pass	Pass		

Opening lead: 6 of hearts

Declarer counts seven winners: three hearts and four clubs. The diamond suit will produce the extra tricks needed for game if South can keep the opponents from switching to the spade suit.

To give West the impression that East has the jack of hearts, South wins the ten of hearts with the king. The king of diamonds is played, then the queen, which West wins. Hoping that the king of spades is the entry for cashing his good hearts after South wins the ace, West returns the three of hearts expecting East to play the jack! Instead, South wins the jack of hearts and makes his game contract plus two overtricks. The Bridge World calls this "a touch of larceny." If South wins the opening lead with the jack of hearts, West will realize that there is no future in the heart suit and he will shift to the three of spades. The defense will win four spade tricks and one diamond to set the game contract.

Mini-lesson: A two notrump opening bid shows 22-23-24 high card points. The hand must be balanced in distribution and all four suits must be protected. The bid is not forcing.

When following suit to a lead, play the lowest of touching equals. For example: Holding AKQ follow with the queen; holding KQJ or QJ follow with the jack; holding QJ10 or J10 follow with the ten.

South dealer
Both sides vulnerable

Deal #39

North
♠ AJ6
♥ Q108
♦ J62
♣ J975

West
♠ 1098
♥ 43
♦ AK974
♣ Q62

East
♠ 75432
♥ 765
♦ 1085
♣ A4

South
♠ KQ
♥ AKJ92
♦ Q3
♣ K1083

South	**West**	**North**	**East**
1 Heart	Pass	2 Hearts	Pass
4 Hearts	Pass	Pass	Pass

Opening lead: King of diamonds

Declarer counts four possible losers: two diamonds and two clubs. A touch of larceny may work! On the opening lead of the king of diamonds, declarer follows with the queen. Afraid to lead the ace and have South trump, making the jack in the dummy good for a possible discard, West shifts to the ten of spades. South wins with the queen, pulls the trumps and discards his losing diamond on the high spade in the dummy. South takes the club finesse which loses to the queen, another club is lost to the ace and South claims his contract, losing one diamond and two clubs.

Mini-lesson: With a 4-3-3-3 distribution, adequate trump support but only three trumps, the responder bids one notrump with six or seven points, gives a single raise of partner's suit holding nine or ten points, and with eight points uses his judgment. Two aces are better than four queens and tens and nines are good fillers and important cards.

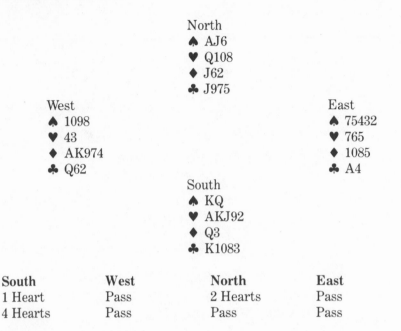

North dealer
East-West vulnerable

Deal #40

North
♠ Q943
♥ 7
♦ KQ53
♣ AJ64

West
♠ 52
♥ AKQ1052
♦ 1042
♣ K2

East
♠ A86
♥ J986
♦ 8
♣ Q10985

South
♠ KJ107
♥ 43
♦ AJ976
♣ 73

North	**East**	**South**	**West**
1 Diamond	Pass	1 Spade	2 Hearts
2 Spades	3 Diamonds*	3 Spades	4 Hearts
4 Spades	Pass	Pass	Pass

Opening lead: 2 of diamonds

Declarer counts three losers: one spade, one heart and one club. With the normal lead of the king of hearts, there is no defense that will set the contract. Declarer will win any shift, drive out the ace of trumps, pull the remaining trumps and concede a club, making four.

With control in spades, the cue bid by East of the opponent's suit* suggests a lead to his partner in case they defend the hand. The bid guarantees a fit in partner's suit; it is the same as raising partner's suit but shows a feature for the defense. With an opening diamond lead, South will be set one trick. When East wins the ace of trumps, he returns a low heart which West wins. West returns a diamond which is trumped by East, and a club trick is collected later in the play.

Mini-lesson: When raising partner's suit, holding four trumps or more, promote the honors in that suit by 1 point. However, there is a limit to the promotion, and if 4 points have already been counted in the trump suit, no promotion takes place.

When raising partner's suit, the distributional points also change. The void suit counts 5 points (instead of 3); the singleton counts 3 points (instead of 2); the doubleton does not change and remains at 1 point.

South dealer
East-West vulnerable

Deal #41

North
♠ Q1062
♥ A6
♦ KQ107
♣ 1095

West
♠ 43
♥ 107432
♦ 983
♣ 76

East
♠ A985
♥ KJ9
♦ A5
♣ J832

South
♠ KJ7
♥ Q85
♦ J642
♣ AKQ

South	**West**	**North**	**East**
1 Notrump	Pass	2 Clubs*	Pass
2 Diamonds	Pass	3 Notrump	Pass
Pass	Pass		

Opening lead: 3 of hearts

Declarer has five winners: two hearts and three clubs. Four tricks must be developed in the spade and diamond suits.

On the opening lead declarer plays the six of hearts and East makes the winning play of the jack. East knows that West does not have a high card point in his hand; South has sixteen points for his notrump opening and between the dummy and his own hand East can count the remaining twenty four high card points in the deck. South wins the jack of hearts with the queen and leads a diamond to the king. East wins the ace and returns the king of hearts which dummy wins. The two of spades is led, East steps up with the ace, returns the nine of hearts which West overtakes with the ten, and he cashes two additional heart tricks to set the contract one trick.

Mini-lesson: *The Stayman Convention is an artificial two club response to an opening 1 notrump bid. Its purpose is to find a four-four major suit fit. The two club response requests partner to bid any biddable major suit. With no biddable four card major suit, the opener bids two diamonds.

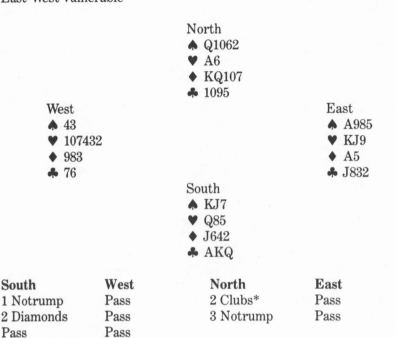

South dealer
Neither side vulnerable

Deal #42

North
♠ J102
♥ 96
♦ K54
♣ KQ1093

West
♠ Q97
♥ AKJ73
♦ A76
♣ 64

East
♠ 8
♥ Q10842
♦ Q1098
♣ 875

South
♠ AK6543
♥ 5
♦ J32
♣ AJ2

South	**West**	**North**	**East**
1 Spade	2 Hearts	2 Spades	3 Hearts
4 Spades	Pass	Pass	Pass

Opening lead: King of hearts

Declarer has four possible losers: one spade, one heart and two diamonds. The overcall at the two level by West would suggest that the ace of diamonds is in that hand. On the king of hearts East plays the two, a signal discouraging a heart continuation. East knows that the declarer has a singleton heart or is void in hearts, for the overcall by West promises a five card or longer suit.

At trick two, West plays the ace of diamonds, East signals with the ten; another diamond lead by West sets up the queen for East and along with the queen of trumps, the defense win four tricks, one spade, one heart and two diamonds.

If West leads anything but a diamond at trick two, declarer will make his game contract.

Mini-lesson: The bid by North is called a free raise. The count for this bid is about 8-11 points.

North dealer
Both sides vulnerable

Deal #43

North
♠ K54
♥ QJ9
♦ 108
♣ Q10764

West
♠ J83
♥ 52
♦ J92
♣ AKJ95

East
♠ Q1092
♥ 63
♦ KQ7543
♣ 2

South
♠ A76
♥ AK10874
♦ A6
♣ 83

North	**East**	**South**	**West**
Pass	Pass	1 Heart	Pass
2 Hearts	Pass	4 Hearts	Pass
Pass	Pass		

Opening lead: King of clubs

Declarer counts four losers: one spade, one diamond and two clubs. Depending upon the defense by East and West, the queen of clubs may set up for a discard of a spade or a diamond loser.

On the lead of the king of clubs, East plays the two.* At trick two, West makes the only play that will defeat the contract . . . a low club which East trumps. South has two additional losers, a spade and a diamond, and is set one trick on good defense.

Mini-lesson: *When the king is led and the queen of that suit is in the dummy, the partner of the leader must play high-low (called an echo) to show a doubleton. Therefore, the two of clubs played by East, shows one or three.

The South hand revalues to 20 points. Review Deal #12.

South dealer
North-South vulnerable

Deal #44

North
♠ Q106
♥ 93
♦ KJ1063
♣ KJ6

West
♠ A73
♥ QJ105
♦ 85
♣ 9542

East
♠ 82
♥ A8742
♦ A72
♣ 1073

South
♠ KJ954
♥ K6
♦ Q94
♣ AQ8

South	**West**	**North**	**East**
1 Spade	Pass	2 Diamonds	Pass
2 Notrump	Pass	3 Spades	Pass
4 Spades	Pass	Pass	Pass

Opening lead: Queen of hearts

Declarer counts three losers: one spade, one heart and one diamond. The opening lead is won by East with the ace. East realizes that the only hope for the defense to win three more tricks to defeat the contract, is for West to have a trump winner and a shortness in the diamond suit. It is unlikely that West has a singleton diamond and a trump winner, for with that holding he probably would have chosen a diamond for his opening lead.

At trick two, East leads the two of diamonds, won by dummy's ten. A low spade is led, the jack losing to the ace in the West hand. West returns a diamond to partner's ace, and a diamond ruff sets the game contract.

Mini-lesson: The two notrump rebid by the opener . . . Review Deal #16.

South dealer
Both sides vulnerable

Deal #45

North
♠ KQ963
♥ 654
♦ K432
♣ 6

West
♠ 84
♥ 82
♦ J986
♣ K10874

East
♠ 2
♥ QJ1073
♦ AQ10
♣ A952

South
♠ AJ1075
♥ AK9
♦ 75
♣ QJ3

South	**West**	**North**	**East**
1 Spade	Pass	4 Spades	Pass
Pass	Pass		

Opening lead: 8 of hearts

Declarer counts four possible losers: one heart, two diamonds and one club. West elected to lead the "top of nothing" in the other major; East follows with the ten and declarer wins with his ace. Two rounds of trumps are led with the ace and king, and the six of clubs is played from the dummy. If East timorously grabs his ace declarer will make his contract. After winning his ace, East returns the queen of hearts, won by South who now plays a "ruffing finesse" with the queen of clubs. If West covers, it will be trumped in the dummy and the losing heart will be discarded on the jack of clubs; if West does not cover, South will discard the losing heart.

If East makes the proper play of a low club when the singleton is led, West will win the king and declarer will not be able to discard his heart loser. This defense will set the contract one trick. If South has the king of clubs, East might lose his ace; however, he will get a heart trick in exchange.

Mini-lesson: The jump by North is called a triple raise. The bid shows five trumps or more, a singleton or a void and no more than 9 high card points. The bid is used for major suits only.

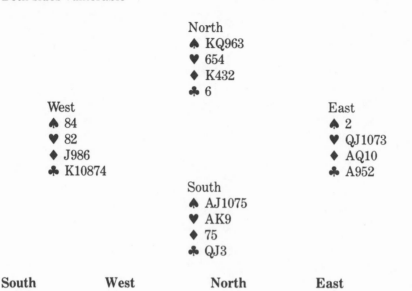

East dealer
Neither side vulnerable

Deal #46

North
♠ J83
♥ 843
♦ J852
♣ AQ3

West
♠ Q6
♥ 102
♦ K109764
♣ 872

East
♠ 74
♥ AKQJ5
♦ 3
♣ J10964

South
♠ AK10952
♥ 976
♦ AQ
♣ K5

East	**South**	**West**	**North**
1 Heart	Double	Pass	2 Diamonds
Pass	2 Spades	Pass	3 Spades
Pass	4 Spades	Pass	Pass
Pass			

Opening lead: 10 of hearts

Declarer counts four possible losers: one spade and three hearts. East wins the opening heart lead with the jack and continues with the king and queen. On the third lead of hearts, West discards his lowest diamond, the four. This discard is a signal to East that West does not want a diamond shift; East can see the two of diamonds in the dummy and the three of diamonds in his own hand. Looking at the clubs in the dummy, there cannot be any future in that suit. At trick four, East leads the ace of hearts; this insures a spade trick for West. If declarer trumps with the nine, West over-trumps; if declarer trumps with the king, the queen will be a winner. This defense sets the contract one trick.

Mini-lesson: The South hand is too strong for a simple overcall of one spade. It is also too strong for an intermediate jump overcall. Strong jump overcalls are no longer used; with a strong hand, a player can make a take-out double and then show his own suit. The bidding by South, doubling and then bidding his own suit at the two level, shows 16-18 points and a good five card or longer suit.

West dealer
East-West vulnerable

Deal #47

North
♠ AQJ107
♥ KQ92
♦ 105
♣ 65

West
♠ 98
♥ 543
♦ A84
♣ AKJ43

East
♠ 632
♥ 7
♦ QJ732
♣ Q1082

South
♠ K54
♥ AJ1086
♦ K96
♣ 97

West	**North**	**East**	**South**
1 Club	Double	3 Clubs	4 Hearts
Pass	Pass	Pass	

Opening lead: King of clubs

Declarer counts four possible losers: two diamonds and two clubs. Unless East and West are knowledgeable players and understand signals, South will make his game contract. Two diamonds can be discarded on the long spades after the trumps have been taken away from the opponents.

On the opening lead of the king of clubs, East plays the ten. At trick two West leads a low club to his partner's queen. East shifts to the queen of diamonds and the defenders win two more tricks, setting the game contract one trick.

Mini-lesson: The play of the ten of clubs by East is called an "equal honor" signal. As the name suggests, the signal is used when partner leads an honor card and you have an honor of equal value.

When you have supported partner's suit, the message is clear; if you want the suit continued, play your next to highest card on partner's honor lead; therefore, the ten denies the jack but promises the queen. If you have not supported partner's suit, your high-low play may show a doubleton.

The jump raise by East over the take-out double . . . Review Deal #36

East dealer
East-West vulnerable

Deal #48

North
♠ Q943
♥ 963
♦ KQJ8
♣ A7

West
♠ 762
♥ J842
♦ 7
♣ 98543

East
♠ A8
♥ AKQ107
♦ 96542
♣ 10

South
♠ KJ105
♥ 5
♦ A103
♣ KQJ62

East	**South**	**West**	**North**
1 Heart	Double	Pass	2 Hearts
Pass	2 Spades	Pass	4 Spades
Pass	Pass	Pass	

Opening lead: 7 of diamonds

The cue bid of the opponent's suit, in response to a take-out double by partner, is the only forcing bid that can be made by the responder. The bid shows about 13 points or more. Holding both major suits, the cue bid may be shaded to 11-12 points. It is a forcing bid and may not be passed until the cue bidder raises partner's suit or bids notrump. A jump in a suit in response to partner's take-out double is not forcing; therefore, the cue bid of the opponent's suit is used to force partner to bid again.

South counts two losers: one spade and one heart. The opening lead is won with the jack. A low spade is led, East steps up with the ace as West follows with the six. East returns a diamond which West trumps with the two (trump echo). West leads the two of hearts won by East with the queen; another diamond is led, West trumps with the seven and the game contract is set one.

Mini-lesson: When a defender plays high-low in the trump suit, either in ruffing or in following to trump leads by declarer, he indicates a holding of three trumps. The signal is used to indicate to partner the ability to ruff a trick.

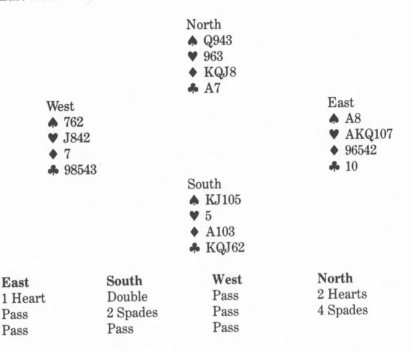

South dealer
North-South vulnerable

Deal #49

North
♠ J4
♥ 10732
♦ KQJ3
♣ Q64

West
♠ K7
♥ Q64
♦ 10874
♣ J1093

East
♠ 85
♥ KJ98
♦ A92
♣ K872

South
♠ AQ109632
♥ A5
♦ 65
♣ A5

South	**West**	**North**	**East**
1 Spade	Pass	1 Notrump	Pass
3 Spades	Pass	4 Spades	Pass
Pass	Pass		

Opening lead: Jack of clubs

Declarer counts four possible losers: one spade, one heart, one diamond and one club. The jack of clubs is covered with the queen, East plays the king and declarer wins his ace. At trick two, South plays a diamond, West follows with the eight (the count signal), the jack is played from the dummy and East does not play the ace. The jack of spades is led for a finesse and West wins the king. West cashes the ten of clubs and South trumps the lead of the nine of clubs. The ace of spades pulls the remaining trumps. A second round of diamonds is led, West follows with the seven, and the queen loses to the ace. East returns a heart, South wins his ace but still must lose one heart and is set one on good defense.

If West plays his lowest card, the four, on the first diamond lead by South, East will play West for an odd number of cards in that suit (three or five) . . . possibly five . . . and win the first lead of diamonds and South will make his game.

Mini-lesson: The count signal is a method by which a defender can indicate to his partner the length held in a particular suit. The procedure is as follows: play high-low with a doubleton; play the lowest from three or five cards; play the second highest card followed by the third highest with four cards.

South dealer
Both sides vulnerable

Deal #50

North
♠ K87
♥ A874
♦ J109
♣ Q98

West
♠ 93
♥ 652
♦ AQ643
♣ K54

East
♠ 10642
♥ KQ9
♦ 872
♣ 763

South
♠ AQJ5
♥ J103
♦ K5
♣ AJ102

South	**West**	**North**	**East**
1 Notrump	Pass	3 Notrump	Pass
Pass	Pass		

Opening lead: 4 of diamonds

Declarer counts his winners: four spades, one heart, one diamond and at least three clubs. The nine of diamonds is played from the dummy, East plays the two (the count signal) and declarer follows with the five. The nine of clubs is led for a finesse and West wins the king. If West doesn't lead the ace of diamonds, South will claim his contract. However, West knows that East has either one diamond or three diamonds from his play of the two at trick one. West cashes his four diamond tricks and sets the contract. If East has a singleton diamond, South has four to the king, and the diamonds in the West hand will not defeat the game.

Mini-lesson: When the dummy wins the first trick, third hand can give his partner the count signal: high-low with two or four; lowest with three or five.

The Stayman Convention is not used when the distribution of the hand is 4-3-3-3.

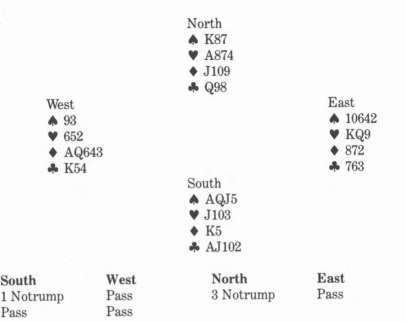

South dealer
East-West vulnerable

Deal #51

North
♠ KJ108
♥ J62
♦ 642
♣ 742

West
♠ 63
♥ Q874
♦ 10873
♣ Q63

East
♠ A742
♥ K105
♦ J9
♣ J1098

South
♠ Q95
♥ A93
♦ AKQ5
♣ AK5

South	**West**	**North**	**East**
2 Notrump	Pass	3 Notrump	Pass
Pass	Pass		

Opening lead: 4 of hearts

Declarer counts six winners: one heart, three diamonds and two clubs. The additional three tricks may come from the spade suit if the defenders win the first or second lead of that suit. One additional heart trick may be developed, depending upon the caliber of the player in the East seat. There may be four diamond winners if the suit breaks evenly.

On the opening lead, the two of hearts is played from the dummy, East properly follows with the ten and declarer plays low. The king of hearts is returned and declarer plays low again. The third heart lead is won with the ace. The queen of spades is led, West follows with the six (the count signal) and East allows the queen to win. South leads another spade, West follows with the three and East plays low again. The spade suit is now useless for lack of entries into the dummy. Declarer cashes two high clubs and three high diamonds and when the diamond suit does not break, the contract is set one trick.

Mini-lesson: The old whist rule of "third hand high" is generally right when a low card is led and the dummy has low cards. However, if dummy has an honor which the third hand player can beat, and that honor is not played, third hand should play his second-highest card if that is a nine or better.

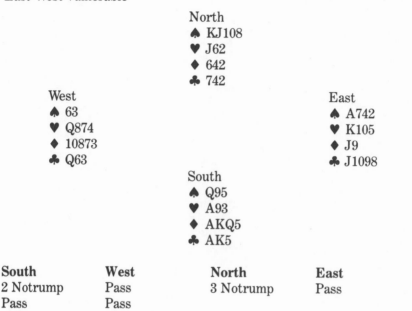

South dealer
North-South vulnerable

Deal #52

North
♠ 10953
♥ K953
♦ AK7
♣ KJ

West
♠ K6
♥ 874
♦ J64
♣ 107432

East
♠ 42
♥ Q106
♦ Q1085
♣ AQ95

South
♠ AQJ87
♥ AJ2
♦ 932
♣ 86

South	**West**	**North**	**East**
1 Spade	Pass	3 Spades	Pass
4 Spades	Pass	Pass	Pass

Opening lead: 3 of clubs

Declarer counts five possible losers: one spade, one heart, one diamond and two clubs. The queen and ace of clubs win the first two tricks and East shifts to the two of trumps; South loses the jack of spades to the king and wins the trump return with the nine in the dummy. The only hope for making the contract is for East to have the queen of hearts and for the suit to break three-three. The losing diamond can be discarded on the thirteenth heart.

The three of hearts is led, East plays the six, declarer follows with the jack which wins. The ace of hearts is led, West and North play low cards and East plays the queen! South leads the two of hearts, West follows with the eight, the nine is played from the dummy and East wins the ten! setting the contract one trick. Larceny on defense!

Mini-lesson: Always play the card that your opponent knows you hold.

Bridge: Teachers Visit Here for Convention and Lectures

BY ALBERT H. MOREHEAD

This has been a week for the nation's bridge teachers to visit New York. The American Bridge Teachers' Association held its annual convention at the Statler-Hilton Hotel on Tuesday and Wednesday, and yesterday, Charles H. Goren's annual course of lectures to bridge teachers began at the Plaza Hotel.

The teachers' convention elected George Gooden of Carmel, California president of the association for the coming year.

The deal shown today was played at the Summer National North American Championships by the newly elected first vice president of the bridge teachers' association, Mrs. D. J. Cook of Winnetka, Illinois.

The contract was a reasonable one, makable if the heart finesse won with some chance to make it even if the finesse lost—a 3—3 heart break, for example, or a doubleton king of spades in East's hand, or other fortuitous circumstances. But it turned out to depend on the classic type of double squeeze, which Mrs. Cook executed handily.

The diamond opening was won by South's king, and South led her low club to dummy's jack so as to lead the heart three and finesse the heart jack.

West won this trick with the heart king and led a second round of clubs, which South took with the king.

South cashed the ace and queen of hearts, for if the suit had been evenly divided there would have been twelve tricks available without further trouble. But the suit did not break.

Then South led her last club to dummy, successfully finessed for the spade king, led her diamond to dummy's queen, and cashed the diamond ace and then the club ace.

This last club lead produced the squeeze on both defenders. East had the high heart and in order to keep it East had to come down to one spade. South then discarded the heart seven. West had the high diamond, which could not be discarded because dummy's diamond eight would then become good, so West too had to come down to one spade. South won the last two tricks with the ace and six of spades.

The only trick the defenders got was the king of hearts and the slam was made.

NORTH
♠ Q54
♥ 93
♦ AQ83
♣ AQJ2

WEST
♠ 1083
♥ K5
♦ J1096
♣ 9743

EAST
♠ K972
♥ 10842
♦ 742
♣ 86

SOUTH
♠ AJ6
♥ AQJ76
♦ K5
♣ K105

Neither side was vulnerable. The bidding:

East	South	West	North
Pass	1 ♥	Pass	2 ♣
Pass	3 N.T.	Pass	6 N.T.
Pass	Pass	Pass	

West led the diamond jack.

'D.J.' Gets 12 Tricks by Astute Play

BY CHARLES GOREN

Neither side vulnerable. South deals.

NORTH
♠ J53
♥ AKQ2
♦ 74
♣ A954

WEST	EAST
♠ 106	♠ KQ2
♥ J853	♥ 10974
♦ J82	♦ Q65
♣ QJ103	♣ K87

SOUTH
♠ A9874
♥ 6
♦ AK1093
♣ 62

The bidding:

South	West	North	East
1 ♠	Pass	2 ♥	Pass
2 ♠	Pass	4 ♠	Pass
Pass	Pass		

Opening lead: Queen of ♣

Coming from the Chicago area and ranking high both as a bridge teacher and tournament player is my good friend D. J. Cook, a lady of great charm. Her father, Carey Orr, is one of the country's leading political cartoonists. "D. J." has carved out a very successful record of her own. In today's hand, she was the only player to score 12 tricks.

Mrs. Cook, seated South, opened the bidding with one spade. When her partner responded with two hearts, she was obliged to rebid the rather mangy spade suit. The alternative call of three diamonds would promise a much better hand. North decided not to dally further and proceeded at once to game in spades.

West opened the queen of clubs. The ace was put up from dummy in order to cash two high hearts, permitting declarer, to discard her club loser. Mrs. Cook crossed over to her hand with the ace of diamonds and led the nine of spades next. West followed with the six, dummy played the three, and East's queen of spades won the trick.

The king of clubs came back and declarer trumped. She now cashed the king of diamonds and then ruffed away the opponent's queen and jack on the next round to establish the diamond suit. The jack of spades was led from dummy, and East was helpless. He actually chose to duck and Mrs. Cook permitted the jack to ride. When the ten dropped from West's hand the contest was virtually over.

Declarer ruffed herself in with a heart, drew East's remaining trump with the ace of spades and played the good diamonds. Her only loser was one trump trick.

NOTES

INDEX

Index

D

There is a *misdeal!* When I recounted the "four decks" of recipes, there were a few extras. There wasn't a one that I wished to relinquish—so I didn't.

Re-Order Additional Copies

Cook And Deal
P.O. Box 3238-Beach Station
Vero Beach, Florida 32960

Please send me ______copies of Cook And Deal at $10.95 per copy plus $1.35 for postage and handling for each book. Florida residents add sales tax.

NAME:______________________________

ADDRESS:______________________________

CITY:______________STATE:__________ZIP CODE________

Cook And Deal
P.O. Box 3238-Beach Station
Vero Beach, Florida 32960

Please send me ______copies of Cook And Deal at $10.95 per copy plus $1.35 for postage and handling for each book. Florida residents add sales tax.

NAME:______________________________

ADDRESS:______________________________

CITY:______________STATE:__________ZIP CODE________

Cook And Deal
P.O. Box 3238-Beach Station
Vero Beach, Florida 32960

Please send me ______copies of Cook And Deal at $10.95 per copy plus $1.35 for postage and handling for each book. Florida residents add sales tax.

NAME:______________________________

ADDRESS:______________________________

CITY:______________STATE:__________ZIP CODE________